D0528867

PLAYING A PART
Drama and Citizenship

PLAYING A PART
Drama and Citizenship

Danny Braverman
with a chapter by Carrie Supple of the
Citizenship Foundation

FALKIRK COUNCIL
LIBRARY SUPPORT
FOR SCHOOLS

Trentham Books
Stoke on Trent, UK and Sterling, USA

Trentham Books Limited

Westview House	22883 Quicksilver Drive
734 London Road	Sterling
Oakhill	VA 20166-2012
Stoke on Trent	USA
Staffordshire	
England ST4 5NP	

© 2002 Danny Braverman (Chapter 1 © Carrie Supple)

All rights reserved. No part of this publication may be reproduced or transmitted in any form or by any means, electronic or mechanical including photocopying, recording or any information storage or retrieval system, without prior permission in writing from the publishers.

First published 2002

British Library Cataloguing-in-Publication Data
A catalogue record for this book is available from the
British Library

1 85856 241 4

© Cover photograph by Dee Conway. Actor Antonia Kemi Coker with Sahin Smyth, Ramoe Mitchell, Angelina Radakovic and Shana Murray from George Mitchell School

Designed and typeset by Trentham Print Design Ltd., Chester and printed in Great Britain by Cromwell Press Ltd., Wiltshire.

Acknowledgements

Writing this book would not have been possible without the support of a number of people. I have drawn on my experiences of almost twenty years working with drama and young people and it's impossible to recall and acknowledge all my colleagues over that period.

I have worked mainly in teams and have frequently collaborated with key individuals who will find their influence to the fore. So thanks are due particularly to Tony Gouveia, Becky Matter and Julia Samuels who have been my partners on countless workshops and programmes of work without which this book could not have been written.

I would like to recognise the contributions of Abigail Amani Chant, Antonia Coker, Tasha Cox, Deni Francis, and Keith Saha for their work on the Theatre Royal's citizenship programmes and to Lou Gray and Dimple Nakum for support with practical ideas in the book.

Carrie Supple and my editor Gillian Klein also deserve special mention, particularly for their encouragement with an author agonising and procrastinating over his first publication.

Lastly, this book was written within the context of my own struggles with ill health. It would certainly not have been possible without the superlative support of my family. So, thanks to my Mum and Dad, Helen and Alan, for sitting by my bedside at the Royal London Hospital ensuring that I ate and elevating the level of conversation; to Jonathan for lunches in Dalston; to Jonah for being the best son in the world; and to Jen for her love and belief in me.

Contents

Foreword

Philip Hedley

For those of us working in British theatre, the new century has plunged us into the most frustrating and the most hopeful of times.

Half the time we theatre directors are drowning in paperwork and worrying whether we really have left no scheme, bursary, grant or potential sponsorship unturned. The other half, we know that some of the principles we value, like social inclusion, multiculturalism and accessibility to the arts are now being championed by the government and we hope we'll find our way through labyrinthine bureaucracy to put those principles into practice effectively.

Nowhere is this contradictory state of affairs more acute and nowhere are the above principles more taken to heart than in the fields of TIE (Theatre-in-Education) and Community Theatre. Both can at their best be enormously effective social tools, and they should be in the front line in creating a sense of community in our towns, especially those plagued by racial tension.

At the Theatre Royal Stratford East we've had more than our fair share of frustrations over the past five years, as, thanks to a Lottery grant, our theatre was closed for major refurbishment. We toured shows locally around East End community centres and youth clubs and even, one week, inside a high-rise block which was in fact the setting of the play. This led me to believe that it would be better for theatres not to have a studio theatre in which they do their experimental work but to develop new shows on the anvil of the youth club tour.

During this time of exile Danny Braverman's work with his education team was bold and innovatory and demonstrated the huge potential for TIE to have a major impact on the teaching of young people and the making of high quality theatre.

Rising to the challenge of starting a new job in a temporarily closed theatre, Danny devised a number of outreach programmes. These projects not only hugely increased our presence in local schools and youth centres but also set alight a wider professional interest in fresh ways of using drama and theatre in educational settings. Danny quickly recognised that, despite the decline in drama in schools, the new Citizenship curriculum could provide the springboard for renewed interest in TIE and youth drama. *Playing a Part* shows us how some of the latest developments in arts education and Citizenship can be focused to bring lasting benefit to young people and their communities.

It has been particularly gratifying for me to see that Danny's work has continued the Theatre Royal's strong tradition of holding education at the heart of our concerns, as originally pioneered by Joan Littlewood and her Theatre Workshop. Joan's most well-known show, *Oh What A Lovely War,* was in many ways the first ever devised TIE show and is still a fine exemplar of education and entertainment going hand in hand. It is perhaps less well-known that Joan instigated our first Youth Theatre and was passionate about linking creativity to learning and developing talent. As *Playing a Part* so ably demonstrates, this way of thinking is still very much with us – maximising the impact of our theatre-work as learning process, uplifting event and inspiring and developing the audience and artists of the future.

Ever since Joan's day, the Theatre Royal's work remains founded on addressing the needs of East London and involving the varied and ever-changing local communities. Paradoxically, this determination to be local has created work which has influenced a wider world. With *Playing a Part,* Danny Braverman has created the opportunity to spread the word about the vital piece of the jigsaw in the future of British theatre: educating and provoking thought in the young.

I was always delighted to go to see *One Thursday* engaging and stimulating its young audiences. The play's inclusion here – alongside the games, exercises and descriptions of projects – allows the book to work on many levels. Each chapter can act as an accessible guide for teachers, youth workers and others to integrate into their own daily practice. But I also hope that *Playing a Part* will do for readers what Danny Braverman's projects have done for the Theatre Royal – inspire us by showing that theatre and drama are superb tools to engage young people in understanding their world – and some of the ways it can be done.

Philip Hedley
Artistic Director – Theatre Royal Stratford East
April 2002

1

The Citizenship Curriculum

Carrie Supple
Citizenship Foundation

Never doubt that a small group of people can change the world...
In fact it is the only thing that ever has. Margaret Mead

In *Playing a Part,* leading Theatre-in-Education practitioner Danny Braverman shows how powerful drama can be in teaching citizenship education of the best kind. Involving children and young people in drama activities engages them with issues at the heart of Citizenship in a powerful and affecting way.

What are the issues? Citizenship has shed its old-fashioned connotations and become a huge umbrella concept. Under its shelter, football clubs promote family literacy; community groups actively challenge entrenched racism; youth clubs prepare to welcome refugees; local councils support intergenerational projects and schools train their students in skills of conflict resolution to reduce bullying.

Citizenship education is good education. Its key values are critical awareness, participation and respect. Contrary to the view that there is citizenship education on the one hand and real education on the other, it seems that in schools where the key values of Citizenship are promoted at the heart of the institution, student motivation is increased and attainment, self-esteem and attendance improve.

On the whole though, schools tend not to be the most democratic institutions and everyone is familiar with the 'Sit down!! Shut Up!! We're going to talk about Human Rights' approach. Unless teaching methods and school structures support and complement the content – learning about democracy, justice and human rights – it will fail. Students must themselves have a living experience of human rights and citizenship education needs to be engaging, lively and fun to stand any chance of success. By the same token, it is no use asking teachers to implement a new curriculum which emphasises consultation and the right to be heard if they feel that their own rights are ignored and they are not listened to or consulted.

It is hard to counter the prevailing culture of judging schools and teachers purely on factual test results, performance indicators and league tables. Those of us advocating citizenship education as a whole school approach are under no illusions about the enormous demands on teachers' time and energy. It is impressive that many schools are able to combine the requirements of the National Curriculum with creative approaches to citizenship education. If citizenship education is seen as a finger wagging, abstract subject, it is doomed. It is not so much a subject, more a way of life and we need to plan in terms of education about, for and through citizenship.

The new Citizenship curriculum enables a vast range of effective practices which have long existed in an ad hoc way to be promoted for all. We are encouraged (at primary level) and required (at secondary) to: encourage young people's active involvement in the life of their school and community; facilitate learning about democracy, social justice and diversity; discuss topical political, spiritual, moral, social and cultural issues and explore methods of effecting social change. The curriculum aims to develop in young people an understanding of themselves as members of society and equip them with the techniques to question and change it for the better. More than that, the final report of the Advisory Group on Citizenship, *Education for Citizenship and the teaching of democracy in schools*, the Crick Report (1998), states, 'We aim at no less than... a change in the political culture of this country' (p.7, 1.5).

The report also identifies certain values and dispositions it considers desirable. They include: determination to act justly; a proclivity to act responsibly, that is, care for others and oneself; concern for human rights and courage to defend a point of view. The new curriculum specifies the importance of developing an ability to empathise, express your own opinions, understand opposing views and reflect on your participation. There is a focus on using group work and building confidence.

The resultant curriculum outlines knowledge, understanding and skills but it does not dictate how we should teach it. Teachers can interpret and deliver the programmes of study as they wish, according to their own local and school needs. This light touch approach has been welcomed by some but not others. Three strands run through Citizenship: political literacy, social and moral responsibility and community involvement, all of which need definition. What exactly is 'community involvement'? It is not clear what the word community means in this context. Many consider the school, as a community in itself, to be an ideal starting place when planning citizenship education. Certain schools are seen as the healthy heart of their communities, others exist as an inaccessible fortress in theirs. All sorts of creative ideas and practice have evolved around the concept but it always sounds easier to facilitate in places teeming with resources and organisations able to facilitate school links. Much more difficult perhaps in areas where the nearest community centre has been burnt down.

Certain commentators who haven't even read the new curriculum, assume it aims to boost nationalism/patriotism/conformity or that this is an initiative to hoodwink (how?) everyone to vote Labour. The gloomiest predictions from those who have read it, are that this curriculum heralds a return to weekly Civics lessons and accompanying tedium. This is a far more justifiable fear than fear of indoctrination. As with any course or resource, everything will depend on how it is introduced to and received by staff.

Some schools have in reality to spend a majority of their time managing behaviour and crises caused by circumstances of which most are beyond teachers' control. So talk of mutual respect and peer-led anti-bullying strategies seems far removed from their reality. On the other hand, it is often in the most desperate-seeming areas that schools become oases of positive and effective practice – because enough people are determined not to let their communities die or the schools implode.

Obviously, without adequate time and cash for appropriate planning, training and resources, effective, quality citizenship education will be very difficult to provide. Although individual teachers can work miracles, teaching in a style which radically affects their students' lives in positive ways, we need to win over more Headteachers and Senior Management Teams. There are many Heads committed to a citizenship education approach who have transformed their institutions into places where mutual respect and collective responsibility are tangible – by working with children, parents and governors

Hundreds of teachers already base their work on the principles of citizenship education. Numerous schools integrated citizenship education as part of their ethos years ago, within a PSHE (Personal, Social and Health Education) programme or in countless other ways – it is certainly not a new concept. It doesn't matter where you start, what matters most is *who* is involved. There are Modern Foreign Language teachers setting up links with Mexican students to discuss Citizenship issues – identity, family, community, rights. There are PE staff and students leading local Show Racism the Red Card campaigns, Year 10 pupils providing peer education for Year 7s who need support in Science, and school caretakers coaching girls' football in response to students' requests. Some schools involve students in the process of appointing staff and shaping rules and sanctions.

In a school aiming to show that all students are capable of taking and showing responsibility, instead of having prefects, the whole of a year group takes turns to help at lunchtime or welcome visitors at reception. And there are the extra-curricular or community based projects which often involve staff working with parents and local voluntary groups. Robert Putnam, in his book *Bowling Alone* (2000), suggests that children who are involved in extra-curricular activities tend to remain active citizens throughout their lives. It takes time to embed citizen-ship education in a school but it can be done. And often there is recognition of the role of art, drama, music and other expressive arts as central to the process. Drama particulary helps us realise that we have to start by examining ourselves and brings to mind Eleanor Roosevelt's words:

> 'Where do human rights begin? In small places close to home – so close and small that they cannot be seen on a world map.'

Many teachers will affirm that using drama – whether in lesson-based role-play or by working with Theatre-in-Education groups – is a powerful and unforgettable way of teaching. Drama can be introduced anywhere, anytime – is not dependent on resources, except for our most precious resource, our own minds, experiences and ideas. At its most effective, drama embraces empathy, thoughts and emotions, group work and communications – all central to citizenship education.

The most successful programmes appeal to the heart as well as the head, engag-ing feelings without manipulation, and this is true for learners of any age. Drama can be an outstanding means of developing key principles of emotional literacy, for instance the idea that we are all in control of our actions; understanding that people are different, experience the world differently, feel and want different things; and that change is possible. A programme which asks children to address crucial issues of identity, community, choices and the roles people play is more likely to succeed if it also encourages learners to be at ease with the language of feelings and opinion.

The play which inspired this book, *One Thursday,* is an outstanding example of drama as an exploration of such complex issues. When it is performed in schools and youth clubs, it works every time, because it is located in a world and in issues that are familiar to the audience, so they listen and can connect. And then they are invited to join in. Like all the best education, it takes us beyond our own experience and makes connections between our lives and the lives of others and asks us to examine key questions of morality and society.

The way the Theatre Royal Stratford East actors work is to encourage their audience to identify aspects of their own lives they'd like to change and suggest that they have a certain degree of choice and can help determine events. Sadly, though understandably, many people believe things happen to them rather than because of them. It is our responsibility to convince the young people we work with that it doesn't have to be that way. The world belongs to them as much as to anyone. They can affect their world if they engage with it and are equipped to become active in a constructive way. Drama helps them to do this. Admittedly, some young people have far more choice than others, but if we use that as an argument for doing nothing, then cynicism and inertia will certainly prevail.

Using *One Thursday* and the techniques Danny Braverman and his team employ can, for example, begin a process of seeing legislation as a means to effect change. Rather than the idea of laws as alien, boring and oppressive, made by faceless people, this approach encourages an understanding of the fact that it is democratically elected people who make laws – often in their own interest, and that the lawmakers and the laws can be changed. Changed in order to benefit the lives of 'ordinary people', as history repeatedly records. Not that laws can change hearts and minds, but they can affect the 'climate' around, for example, attitudes towards human rights or equality of opportunity. We are all able to operate more effectively as citizens if we understand how the law is made and operates and how it affects us.

In the words of Andrew Phillips, a founder and now President of the Citizenship Foundation:

> The gap between the citizen, the law and those who make and enforce it is relentlessly widening. That so easily breeds resentment together with a dangerous disengagement from any sense of ownership of, or participation in, civil society and its institutions.

The organisation, started in 1989 to teach young people about their rights and the law, covers all aspects of Citizenship – education for democracy, human rights, political literacy and social and moral responsibility. Part of the lobby for citizenship education to be a compulsory part of the curriculum, it now supports schools in their implementation of the orders. This is often done in partnership with other like-minded organizations or groups such as Danny Braverman's team. The main aim of Citizenship as a new subject is to encourage connections between people and their communities – school, local, national and international. Knowing about how systems work or knowing how to find out, gives young people more power and helps them call their elders to account and deal with disappointments.

The Foundation has produced resources and activities which facilitate discussion based, experiential learning, bringing the otherwise potentially dry components of Citizenship alive. As examples of using drama to develop citizenship action, our youth parliament and mock trial competitions encourage students to explore the way these institutions work and the meaning of concepts such as justice, impartiality, evidence and bias in an active and enjoyable way. Eddie Parkinson, former head of History at Kenton School in Newcastle upon Tyne, wrote this about entering his students for the Bar Mock Trial:

> I have never been involved in anything else that has demolished the low self-esteem which afflicts so many bright working class pupils quite as effectively. I would also stress that that burgeoning confidence in public speaking, refined skills in the selection and use of evidence and an acute awareness of the importance of teamwork are advantages when applied across the curriculum.

Many professionals working with young people use elements of drama, with role-plays/mock trials, theatrical youth parliaments etc. to great effect and we hope that this book will support the introduction of more drama into their work and develop their students' confidence and real active participation (see Chapter 8).

If we want young people to develop an inclination to think for themselves and to respect and speak out on behalf of others we need to focus on the most effective methods of achieving this. To be effective, we need to reach deep – and this is difficult to achieve within the existing curriculum, but it can be done.

A student watching the testimony of a Holocaust survivor said that the words had 'got inside' her. Readers will have experienced other incidents. In 1992 when the war in Bosnia was raging, most students in my class were Muslim. They felt angry and hurt by what they saw as the lack of a humanitarian response towards those who were suffering in Bosnia. We talked about the few people who had risked their lives to hide and save victims of the Nazis and why so few had done so. 'Miss' said one boy, 'if they thought it was their business, they would have done something.'

The Holocaust may sometimes be an inappropriate reference point for human behaviour because its circumstances were so extreme. But central to citizenship education is the concept of whether we see it as our 'business' to think and care and act to support other people. Drama can make this real by asking students to see as others see and feel, and can do so in a non-threatening way. Young people need to be given opportunities to think, talk, question and act.

Too many events featuring young people are not truly a result of joint decisions or consultation but instead use them tokenistically, as decoration. Article 12 of 1989 United Nations Convention on the Rights of the Child states that children have a 'right to express themselves freely in all matters considering them' and that their views should be given proper consideration. Many committees of adults working in the field of Citizenship might have the best intentions regarding children's rights and participation but end up speculating about what might be of interest to young people, rather than ensuring they are there in the first place as part of the organisation or that they are at least consulted directly.

Just because a group of adults who wrote the Citizenship curriculum think it important for everyone to understand their rights and responsibilities and the 'System', why should our children think so too? And how can we engage and maintain their interest? We need to consult and review the content and methodology of our work, in partnership with students wherever possible.

The new curriculum is sometimes described as 'preparation for Citizenship' but this implies that young people are not yet citizens and it also denies crucial aspects of existing citizenship education in action. While the popular image of school age students is usually either of irresponsible and dangerous hoodlums or vulnerable little people in need of protection, the reality is vastly more complex. Those who complain about 'young people today' would be amazed to see some of the hundreds of outstanding initiatives thriving in the UK alone, such as the winners of the Philip Lawrence Awards for outstanding youth led citizenship initiatives. Recent examples include Nil By Mouth, a Glasgow group opposing sectarianism in sport and Youth Liaison Volunteers in Bournemouth, a peer education project working to reduce violence and drug abuse associated with night clubs in the town.

This enthusiasm and drive to work for positive social change is happening in the same society that, we are told, is becoming increasingly selfish and within which there are crises of identity, community and democracy. We urgently need to identify the factors which explain the success of projects promoting active community life. Meanwhile, we should try to nurture the belief that we are all responsible for each other and that, in the words of Martin Luther King, 'Injustice anywhere is a threat to justice everywhere.'

This book offers a tremendous variety of approaches for teachers and youth workers who want to include drama in their work. Rather than providing a blueprint for correct practice, Danny Braverman writes in a way which will encourage people to devise their own strategies. Having seen the responses to performances of *One Thursday* in schools and youth clubs, it is clear that the ideas, games, activities, anecdotes and schemes of work in this book offer an original way into tackling some of the most challenging and vital aspects of citizenship education.

References

Education for Citizenship and the teaching of democracy in schools. Final report of the Advisory Group on Citizenship (1998) Tel. 01787 884444

Hannam, Derry (2001) *Pupil Voice and Democracy – a report based on attitudes, attainment, attendance and exclusion in secondary schools that take student participation seriously: a pilot study research in collaboration with CSV, funded by the DfES.* Derry Hannam is Project Director of The Phoenix Trust derry@demos51.freeserve.co.uk

Putnam, Robert (2000) *Bowling Alone: The Collapse and Revival of American Community.* Simon and Schuster

2

Why Drama and Citizenship?

A few years back, while working as Education Director at the Theatre Royal Stratford East in London, I received a letter from Waltham Forest Youth Service inviting me to create a project embracing the new 'citizenship' agenda. My initial reaction was to decline politely. At first it seemed that a project of this nature was intrinsically unworkable. My cynicism suggested that the primary motivation for such a venture was to find an attractive way to persuade the next generation of voters to turn out for elections. From the point of view of the state, this is an urgent problem. Statistics tell us that young people are very alienated from the voting process and therefore, as the years go on, turn-out will surely decline drastically. 71 per cent of 16–21 year olds are reported as saying that, whoever they vote for, it will make no difference to their lives (Hertz, 2001) and so our politicians have an increasingly shaky mandate. Although a theatre project might seem, on the surface, a useful tool to tackle this problem, I was concerned that the root causes of 'voter apathy' would not be addressed.

In truth, I have a great deal of sympathy with young people who choose not to exercise their democratic right to vote. From the point of view of a first-time voter particularly, the political parties appear much the same. The political class, by and large, do not reflect the communities they serve and seem to communicate in pedantic and elusive ways. Most importantly, our voting model is based on the notion of *representation* not *participation*. In many constituencies, using your vote to increase accountability is seen as pointless when the representative's seat is 'safe'. In addition, politicians whose rhetoric stresses their ability to listen to their constituents lack credibility set against a climate of sleaze and when everyday experience tells us that so little has changed in our material circumstances.

Despite these misgivings, I phoned Vicki Cotton, Waltham Forest's Head of Youth Service, to chat further about the project. In the course of our conversation, it became clear to me that there was potential to use drama and theatre in partnership with a local council. As I outlined the ethos and methods of our work, a common approach emerged. Emphatically, our project would not follow the model of a didactic programme of work emphasising a citizen's duty to vote. Rather, we would stress the state's responsibility to be accountable to its citizens. In this respect, drama and theatre can be very useful. Stories of the everyday impact of the state on people's lives can be told, an exchange of views can be facilitated by appreciating a range of perspectives from within a role, and confidence to present your ideas can be built through performance techniques.

The realisation of these ideas became a project entitled 'Making a Difference'. It took a number of forms – workshops, performances and forums. Young people engaged politicians and other key policy-makers on their own terms and useful exchanges started the process of creating real change. At the time of writing, this idea is still in its infancy in the UK. However, pockets of activity all over the world – notably inspired by Augusto Boal's experiments with Legislative Theatre in Brazil – indicate that this is a good idea whose time has come.

As we toured schools and youth clubs with the project, interest was sparked in many quarters interested in the practicalities of how to deliver the new citizenship curriculum in schools and informal education. Carrie Supple from the Citizenship Foundation came to see us working with young people and, inspired by what she saw, encouraged me to share our work more widely by writing this book. Carrie has contributed a chapter, putting the rest of it in the context of the new curriculum. The result of the whole book, I hope, will be to share understanding and techniques with professionals charged with the task of teaching citizenship.

My aim is to provide a resource that is both a practical tool and an inspiration to develop practice more widely. Drama specialists may find fresh approaches and the ideas in the book may encourage those new to drama to try theirs out. Chapter Three is the best place to start if you're not very familiar with drama. The games and exercises described there offer an experiential approach that can be adapted to a variety of circumstances and fed in to different schemes of work on a number of issues. Chapter Four is the play text we used in 'Making a Difference'. When we toured the play *One Thursday*, it was often remarked that the play itself would be a useful resource for young people. The play has been edited to allow maximum flexibility for use in either a classroom or youth centre. It can accommodate different cast sizes and be used effectively as three short (fifteen minute) plays. Chapter Five offers a range of follow-up ideas for use with the text. These ideas are not exclusive to *One Thursday* and can be adapted for use with a number of relevant texts. Chapters Six and Seven look at young people creating their own plays through devising and writing. Chapter Six suggests ways to get the devising process started and Chapter Seven offers case studies of a variety of citizenship projects. Chapter Eight concludes the book by proposing a model of work to use drama to create and sustain youth parliaments and forums.

It's been difficult to define the parameters of the book. After all, most drama and theatre practice can be adapted to address citizenship concerns. In particular, I've omitted any in depth description of the process of creating and animating Forum Theatre, even though I've used it as a primary strategy. The bibliography will guide readers to some of the growing body of literature on the subject and other related topics.

Although there's a variety of definitions of the difference between drama and theatre, this book makes a distinction that may be useful for educational purposes. The term 'drama' is used to describe the kind of 'process' work that doesn't necessarily demand an audience, and 'theatre' an event that requires both an audience and a separated space to create a performance. Both modes may well be present in a workshop, as – say – work in small groups is shared with a larger group.

The sense of being someone else is present in many complex ways during both drama and theatre work. Even as audience, we're often imagining what it's like to be the person depicted in front of us. It is in this interplay between our own experience and the parallel experience of an imagined other that the educational value of the work is found.

The drama and theatre methods in this book are founded particularly on three central notions about how this act of pretending to be someone else is of educational value – particularly when teaching citizenship.

Empathy

Facing the audience at Winchester prison, we were scared. The Forum Theatre piece 'Looks' was a project run by LEAP – a Quaker-founded youth arts organisation concerned with conflict resolution – and explored how physical appearance has an impact on the quality of our lives. The narratives were true stories about racism, homophobia and eating disorders. The team of young trainees who had created the programme was mixed in terms of gender, race and sexuality. In the front row of the audience, in amongst a sea of perplexed, white, male faces sat two skinheads complete with swastika and union jack tattoos. The clash of cultures was raw and our fear unsurprising.

The prison officer, by way of trying to steady our nerves, had let us know that although there were a number of young men imprisoned for violence – football hooliganism and the like – he was assured of their good behaviour. We explained to him that we wanted not just to present the theatre piece but also to encourage the audience to participate in the drama. Would this be safe? He let us know that fierce retribution and withdrawal of privileges would counter any misdeeds. The team remained sceptical.

We were playing a scene where a young male protagonist was rowing with his Dad about his decision to wear make-up, when we came across an unexpected response. We were used to lively audiences of young people engaging with and commenting on the action, but never had we had such a wave of sympathy for the boy with make-up. During the interaction that followed the show, several young men took the place of the protagonist and argued in role with his authoritarian father, putting the case eloquently for the right to wear make-up. The image of a skinhead with a swastika tattoo on his face proclaiming his right to wear mascara because 'it's the person inside that matters' will never leave me. Somehow the structure of this theatre experience had helped this young man to step into the shoes of an overtly 'effeminate' character – perhaps for the first time.

A major aspiration of citizenship education is to support and develop young people's innate abilities to discuss and negotiate. In this respect particularly, empathy is an essential value to promote. By contrast, the culture of much adult political activity encourages antagonism and the battle of entrenched positions. So by promoting empathy as a positive value, we are also encouraging the next generation to challenge the prevailing methods of decision-making. To help young people to engage empathetically with their peers, we should encourage imaginative approaches, particularly the ability to imagine oneself as someone entirely different. Nowhere is this more vital than in challenging prejudice.

Drama is clearly a strategy that can create the circumstances to make that imaginative leap into the thoughts and feelings of other people. Drama activity can uniquely enable a participant to shed much of the day to day habitual opinions and attitudes that can inhibit honest scrutiny of any issue. After all, on a surface level the activity of enacting another person's life is playful. We are all accustomed to the fact that a purpose of drama is to strive for artistic truth and authenticity and that to achieve this to maximum effect, we must reach a greater understanding of the feelings, social conditions and interpersonal relationships of a 'character'.

Inevitably, to be effectively empathetic, we tend to recognise something of ourselves in the characters we play – much as I imagine the inmate at Winchester prison did – and imagination enables us to build further belief in the drama from this simple starting point.

Playfulness

Much has been written about the relationship between drama and play, and I won't attempt to re-cover too much old ground here. However, the title of this book – *Playing a Part* – is intended to draw attention to the way we use the word play to evoke a range of associated meanings. It's also a gentle challenge to the culture in many learning environments, where 'play' is experienced as the re-creational alternative to 'study'. In our context, playfulness is an intrinsic part of a valuable learning experience.

Within meaningful play events seriousness and creativity are often bound together. The play we go to the theatre to see and the play we enjoy in the park are both rule-bound events within which creativity can flourish. It may require an idealistic mental leap to perceive the 'part we play' in our community in the same light. However, closer scrutiny of, say, the House of Commons or, indeed, a lively local tenants association meeting or youth parliament will reveal the players struggling to employ their creative muscles to reach understandings and to enliven their decision-making.

Playfulness – which implies a sense of fun – is sadly lacking in many political and theatre events. Perhaps it's deemed synonymous with frivolity. However, lack of playfulness might well be at the root of young people's dissatisfaction with both theatre and politics – both arenas being perceived as over-earnest and boring. A sense of playfulness can, however, help to immerse players in an otherwise unappealing activity. At the present time, with teachers and other educators concerned about how to deliver a potentially 'boring' curriculum, strategies that authentically engage young people are at a premium.

Playfulness motivates people through their innate sociability to participate in collective activity, whilst maintaining a focus on what's at stake. A discussion format frequently poses depersonalised questions, e.g. 'what are the results of poverty?' A playful approach, particularly within a dramatic framework, encourages a more open and experiential response, e.g. 'what would you do if you were Shaheen and you only had a handful of coins left for the rest of the day?' This is explored in more depth in Chapters 4 and 5.

I hope this book is suffused with the spirit of playfulness. In terms of drama work, the group-leader who encourages the key elements of playfulness – lack of judgement of others, willingness to experiment and mutual respect – will be supporting authentic, spontaneous and courageous responses from their group.

A spirit of playfulness is encouraged in this book through the choice of terminology. Where possible, I have used the term 'player' to denote a participant in any activity. For me, a player is many things rolled into one – a performer, a learner, an activist, a participant, a negotiator, an advocate and an artist.

From the particular to the universal

This phrase, borrowed from Dorothy Heathcote (Wagner, 1979), underpins the learning methods in this book. At the heart of the drama and theatre experiences described is the importance of building belief in a parallel, fictional world. This fictional world is designed to resonate with the everyday experiences of the players. Sometimes this will mean the observation of or participation in activities that mirror contemporary existence – such as acting out the play *One Thursday*. At other times the fiction may have an historical or fantastical context. Nevertheless, on every occasion the focus will be on an enclosed world of human characters interacting – on their feelings and actions as well as their belief systems.

Once an interesting dramatic framework has been introduced, the key skill for any group-leader is to – in Heathcote's words – 'drop to the universal'. The universals are often those prescribed by the citizenship curriculum in schools or other social objectives within the youth service or other informal settings. Some of the questions raised will dig below the surface into fundamental questions of human rights; e.g. following a performance of Mikey's story in *One Thursday*, the group look at a child's right to education. Does that include the right to have a private space to do homework? Other universal questions will be moral or ethical, e.g. in Femi's story in *One Thursday* a group might look at the general dilemma of how far your loyalty to a friend will stretch.

In terms of addressing issues of political literacy, it's worth highlighting the impact of the state on the lives of particular characters. In a way, the state becomes a player in the drama and universal issues of the impact of government on our lives can be drawn out. The workings of parliament or local government – not always of direct interest to young people – can thus become an urgent element of the equation. In the course of experimenting with drama and citizenship work, it often surprised me how little connection was made between government and day to day experiences. There seems to me to be little awareness of channels of accountability; the way an individual interacts with, say, their GP, teacher or housing officer appears to be detached from the laws and statutes that govern their activity. I employed a useful catch-phrase to address this deficit: 'you're an expert in your own life'. This phrase is designed to empower people to imagine that they can effect the fundamental workings of the state.

This is not the same as the classic drama strategy of the 'mantle of the expert' (see Neelands, 1990). By contrast to donning a 'white coat' and imagining yourself to have specialist knowledge, there is recognition that – just by being a citizen who is affected by the state – you have enough knowledge to participate in decision-making. Hence, a key strategy to bring out the political universals inherent within any particular experience is the promulgating of new laws and policies. The final chapter of this book looks at the potential for using drama to build a more participatory democratic process based on this principle.

Group-leaders will often wish to guide a drama process towards the exploration of particular universals they themselves deem important or that are part of a larger scheme of work, such as the citizenship curriculum. It's worth noting that drama and theatre experiences don't always elicit predictable responses – and this is what often gives them their unique value.

Following a performance of *One Thursday* at Brampton Manor School in Newham, I was facilitating a post-show discussion with a group of young white women who were particularly animated about the character Femi's conflict with the police. I explained to the group that I would like to try and summarise the session by having them create a list, based on their own experiences, titled 'Something should be done about...'. Before that, however, could they talk about which elements of the play had most connected with their own experience? Clearly the play had not led this group down the more familiar path of exploring universal questions of race discrimination and prejudice.

'The police harass us too.'

'We're just standing around and they come and give us grief.'

'Do you know why?' I asked.

'Yeah, the clothes we wear. If you wear a hoody and baggy trousers they think you've committed a crime.'

'Just because of the clothes you wear?' I ventured.

'Yeah, but if you wear like a skirt or something then some man'll beep you in his car.'

'So, there's no clothes you can wear that won't get you in trouble?'

'That's right.'

'Put that down.. something should be done about men harassing girls in public. Grown men in their cars, y'know!'

From that point of white girls identifying with the story of a black boy, the group went on to discuss animatedly their own experiences of feeling unsafe on the streets. They had also opened up a whole world of wider issues – gender differences, the state's responsibility to protect them and the rights of young people in general. They were also, now, primed to promulgate actual changes that should be made to alleviate the problem and prepared to take this on to their school council and local youth parliament.

3
Games and Exercises

If you've not done it before, I recommend observing young people intent on playing a game. It can be any game – a handheld computer game, a sporting match or simply an impromptu game of tag in a playground. Particularly, watch the non-verbal communication – the facial expressions and the body movement – and the complex and intense range of emotions displayed. What you'll often observe is a quality of absorption and commitment to a task rare in most educational activities. At one level the player is being elevated from the distractions and stresses of everyday existence – recreation is both intensely serious and great fun. Often this experience is also accompanied by a dramatic frame of mind – experiencing what it might be like to be someone different for a moment or two. It's therefore clear to see why game-playing is a fundamental tool for drama workshops.

The games and exercises described in this chapter are offered as useful beginnings for the exploration of citizenship issues. In the main, they're structures for players to engage with broad themes and they're flexible enough to be adapted for a specific group's needs and for a variety of contexts. If there is an overarching aim, it's to encourage a genuine absorption – whether generated by the group themselves or by its leader.

These games, exercises and their follow-on sequences are ideally used to kick off further drama work. They have the power, if handled sensitively, to release inhibitions and foster appropriately focused energy. There's also a degree of security for a group-leader, as most of these games will produce a fairly predictable range of responses. In essence, they ritualise fundamental human experiences such as power, status, territory and conflict. They also have the potential to acclimatise your group to a learning area – relaxing players by diminishing the residual effects of the previous lesson or a row with a friend. For many people, the ways of the drama workshop are unfamiliar, particularly the requirement to engage wholeheartedly with group work. These games and exercises are examples of a bridge into the kinds of drama and theatre work found elsewhere in this book.

As with many children's games, drama operates on two complementary levels. On the surface a player is intent on a simple goal, such as producing a convincing mime, passing a signal or winning a competition. On a subconscious level, feelings and issues are being explored. This duality is unusual in more formal educational settings where learning outcomes are prescribed as pre-determined targets. By contrast, the emotional and thematic content of drama games lends itself to open learning, and is therefore ideal for exploring citizenship where there may be no obvious or objective 'right answer' to a moral or ethical question.

The physical and emotional activity of playing games provides a group with a communal experience as the starting point for their work and often engenders a celebratory atmosphere. But it's important to give ample time for plateaux of reflection, so the group can consider their interpretation of events and start to develop a rounded understanding of any given topic.

It's also useful to consider a variety of interesting ways to encourage reflection. As well as varied discussion formats, the group can consolidate their learning in other ways, such as individual and group writing, drawing and other drama formats.

I've also indicated in this chapter how the games and exercises can function as inspiration for follow-up sequences. This is by no means intended to be prescriptive, but just indicates the potential for designing drama sessions coherently.

Sheriff

Sheriff is a game that explores the theme of violence. It resonates with familiar TV and film formats, providing an opportunity for your group to engage physically and emotionally with a hot topic, within the safety of a game.

The group stands in a circle with one player, the sheriff, in the middle. The sheriff mimes shooting at someone in the circle and shouts 'bang!' That person then ducks and the players either side mime shooting at each other whilst shouting 'bang'!. The sheriff decides whose reactions were the quickest and they are declared the winner. The loser sits down and is now 'out'. The game continues in this vein until there are only two players left. They then stand back to back, as if it were an old-fashioned duel. The sheriff then starts to count, deliberately missing out a number ('one. two.. three.. five!'). This is the signal for the two remaining players to turn and mime shooting. The sheriff declares the quickest player as the winner, who then becomes the sheriff for the next round.

Following a lively game of Sheriff, the leader asks the group to describe their feelings during the game:

'I wasn't concentrating, so I was out early. It was a real shock!'

'I was angry, because I thought I'd won. But the sheriff made me sit down!'

'I was really aware, on my toes, so that I felt I could beat anyone on either side.'

'I loved being the sheriff. Real power!'

'I didn't like being the sheriff. I didn't want to make a decision to have someone out of the game.'

Leader: 'Was this similar to any real violent situations?'

'That feeling that anything could happen, it's a bit like that just walking across the park, even if nothing happens to you, you're worried something might.'

'You have to be really aware that people can attack you in certain situations.'

'And some people are like the sheriff... the police... the army... They have to make life and death decisions.'

'And sometimes it's like the person being shot at. If you avoid the violence, your mate gets it.'

'Yeah... and it can be really embarrassing being the victim of violence. You can look really weak.'

Follow-on sequence

Already the group has offered fragments of narrative. These can now be the starting points for further drama.

Recap on the dramatic situations discussed at the end of the game (e.g. walking late at night through the park, being embarrassed by being the victim of violence, being the person making a life and death decision).

Ask them to prepare, in small groups, a short scene with one of these situations as a starting point. Their task is to focus on one central character. The scene is to be performed without dialogue, focusing on body language and expression. The only words to be used are those that track the thoughts of the central character.

Share the scenes and discuss. Could this scene occur anywhere in the world? Are some places and societies less violent than others? Could these conflicts be resolved or managed better? What can governments do to reduce these violent situations?

The game of power

This game is adapted from an exercise by Augusto Boal (1992).

The Game of Power is particularly useful for groups who may be a bit nervous about drama, as the initial 'actors' in the exercise are pieces of furniture!

Take six chairs, a bottle and a table. Ask the players, in small groups, to create a sculpture using only those objects to create a scenario in which one of the chairs is made the most powerful.

The whole group reflects on what they see.

*   Which chair is the most powerful?

*   What else do you see? Is there a second most powerful chair? Which is the least powerful object?

*   If the objects were people, who might they be?

*   Does the sculpture remind you of any specific situations?

Then invite someone to change one of the chairs. How does this change the situation?

One group places the table on its four legs with an upright chair by its side facing towards the other chairs. These other chairs are lined up away from the table, with three in a row facing the other two. The bottle is on the table next to the first chair.

The first and most obvious interpretation is that this is a waiting room and the chair next to the table is the one with the greatest power.

The group builds on each other's contributions.

'That's the receptionist at the doctor's, the bottle is her microphone'

'The other chairs are sick people waiting to be seen'

'They don't know who's next.'

'Yes... It's not first come, first served.'

'She chooses, the receptionist chooses who goes when.'

'Why? That's not fair!'

'She likes her power... the doctor doesn't treat her well... She takes it out on the patients.'

The group continues to discuss the dynamics of this situation, quite naturally giving character and story to the inanimate objects. They discuss why the receptionist uses a microphone, the feelings of the patients and whether there is an absent someone else (i.e. the doctor) with more power in this situation.

The leader asks the group if anyone has any ideas for changing just one object to create a different sense of power. One young man takes one of the 'waiting' chairs and tips it over so that it's leaning against its neighbour.

'That's a sick child with his mum.'

'Yes, and for some reason she's waiting longer.'

'Nobody believes the child is ill.'

There's a pause.

'Especially his mum.'

The strength of the Game of Power is that a group projects human qualities onto the objects. As such, it functions as a way to unearth the latent concerns and interests of a group and thus motivates players into involving themselves in the session.

This Game of Power will tend to lead to two different types of sculpture. One will lend itself to a *naturalistic* interpretation, a familiar scene or situation, as in the example above. The other will be *abstract*, symbolising something important to the group. In this instance, the physical placement of the objects will not instantly suggest an actual scene.

To develop from a naturalistic starting point, the leader can simply add characters to the scene, treating the sculpture as a stage setting.

Players are invited to become still characters in the scene, emphasising the importance of accurate facial expression.

The scene is brought back to life with a click of the fingers, to see what happens next.

The scene is replayed with different power dynamics. For example, the doctor's waiting room scene is further explored by inviting one character to complain about the service. A research project is proposed into existing mechanisms for complaining about health issues.

To develop from a symbolic starting point, the group-leader works with the group to deconstruct the image:

Names are proposed for the sculpture. Start with names that evoke feelings (e.g. 'humiliation', 'anger', 'control'). How might this sculpture say something about our society? What about names for the sculpture that begin with 'the power of...' (e.g. 'the power of the military' 'the power of the law' 'the power of money')?

Once it's established that the sculpture could be a depiction of something we all understand, individuals are invited to adopt a still image that shows a feeling or attitude towards the subject. For example, if it's decided that the sculpture is titled 'the power of the military', one person might depict 'bravery', another 'dissent' and another 'fear'.

The sculpture is dismantled and a topic has been established for further work.

There are a number of alternative ways of adapting the Game of Power to match a variety of needs:

If you're working in a confined or cluttered space, try creating 'table-top' sculptures. Instead of the chairs, use audiocassette cases; use a book instead of the table and a bottle top instead of the bottle.

Once the game has been played in its original form, the group will have it as part of its drama vocabulary. This means you can play it again, but with a given theme. For example, the group is looking at different forms of government. Small groups are given cards to create their own furniture sculptures (e.g. 'parliamentary democracy', 'totalitarianism', 'anarchy', 'apartheid' etc). This time, the group is allowed to select new objects to create their sculpture. This encourages discussion about the topic (e.g. what object might you choose to represent a 'dictator'? What will that communicate to your 'audience'?). Once the sculpture has been planned, the whole group can view the results and try to guess the word(s) on the card. This naturally leads on to further work on assessing the values and ethics of each system of government.

Numbered chairs

This sequence of games and exercises sets up a ritual of responses using the simple mechanism of a row of chairs. This starts with a competitive game requiring quick responses and focused attention. Once the ritual is established, the group-leader can feed in appropriate content.

A line of chairs equal to the number of players is set up in a room, numbered in sequence. Each player sits in a chair. The game starts with number one, who stands up and declares their number followed by another number. The person with the second number then stands up and follows suit. The group-leader adds two rules to make the game more challenging. Players are not allowed to use an adjacent number (e.g. '1...2!') or to go back to the person who just chose you (e.g. '1... 5' '5...1'). In addition, the group-leader makes it clear to number one that the last number is also next to them. So if there are fifteen chairs in a line, number fifteen is next to number one for the purpose of the game. If any player makes a mistake – which usually includes slowness or fumbling – then that player goes to the last chair and everyone else shuffles up a space. The number remains with the chair, not the player. The aim of the game is to 'get' number one!

This game provides a physical and enjoyable experience to introduce the idea of status in its broadest sense. Mostly, the player who manages to stay in number one chair the longest will gain the highest status in the group.

Follow-on sequence

To move the session on, the group-leader uses the format of the row of numbered chairs to explore a variety of personal positions and their implications for citizenship.

The players are now given a series of instructions, which will end up with them choosing one of the chairs. They will need to consider their responses in silence without conferring. They should also be bold and unhesitant in making choices. On some occasions a number of players will gravitate towards the same seat. In that instance, the players are encouraged to queue up behind the seat corresponding to their response.

Leader: 'Consider the death penalty. Chair number one represents the view that there are a great many occasions when the death penalty should be used (e.g. for any murder or manslaughter, rape, torture, kidnapping). The last chair represents the view that it is never justified. The other chairs represent, in order, all the shades of opinion in between. Go to the chair that most closely represents your opinion.'

The group spreads out amongst the chairs.

Leader: Give me one sentence each to say more about your opinion. Everyone can say one thing and no one's allowed to interrupt. There'll be room for more discussion later.

'I went right to the end because I believe that it is never justified to take a life.'

'I went to the one nearly on the end, because I thought it was right that the Nazis were executed, but I can't think of any other circumstances.'

'I went to number three because I thought that there are some people who have a right to self-defence and may have to kill, but otherwise it would be a deterrent.'

'I went to number one because I believe in an 'eye for an eye'.'

The group-leader asks each player to imagine that they're now someone from their parents' generation. It could be their mum or dad, or equally a neighbour, teacher or acquaintance. The previous exercise is then repeated in role, including the one line responses.

The group is paired off and asked to discuss the issue whilst staying in role, trying to persuade their partner to their point of view.

The group is then invited to repeat the chair exercise for a third time, this time choosing a character with a direct investment in the issue (e.g. in the death penalty example, a prisoner on death row, the parent of a murder victim, a holocaust survivor, a gun manufacturer etc). Again, a pair discussion exercise takes place in role.

In reflection, the whole group is now invited to discuss the issue out of role:

- Which characters did you feel closest to or furthest from?

- Did any of the characters' views alter your personal position? Were any characters more persuasive than others? Why?

- Which chair do you think represents the average view of the British public? Does this differ, say, from the view of newspapers, the government of this country or governments of other countries?

- How difficult is it to express an opinion outside the mainstream?

To close the exercise, the group goes to chairs that represent their current view, given their experience of the session. Have there been any changes of opinion?

This exercise can be adapted to explore any number of issues, particularly where it's useful to uncover shades of opinion (e.g. about immigration – from no barriers to repatriation; drug laws – from total legalisation to prohibition of alcohol and tobacco).

Arrange yourself

This game is particularly useful for groups who enjoy a competitive edge to games, but who may need support with teamwork, listening and working instinctively.

The group is divided into teams of eight to twelve people, who are asked to line up one behind another. The leader then tells the group that there will be a series of instructions. Each team must complete an instruction accurately and then sit down. The first group to be sat down, with the instruction accurately completed, wins a point. Points are recorded on a simple scoreboard and a winning team announced.

The key to this game is to use the structure to move from simple physical instructions to instructions that require discussion and that ultimately contain content to explore a topic, for example 'the media'.

The series of initial instructions might be:

Arrange yourselves according to...

... height with the tallest at the back.

... shoe size with the smallest at the back.

... how many brothers and sisters you've got (including step- and half-brothers and sisters) with the most at the front.

... your house number, with the highest at the back and with a house 'name' counting as 0.

The next set of instructions can explore the players' relationship to the media and media representation:

Arrange yourselves according to...

... the number of hours you spend per week in front of a screen.

... the number of television channels you can receive in your home.

... the number of websites you visited in the past month.

... the number of radio stations you listen to regularly.

... the number of newspapers you've read all or part of in the past month.

The exercise is now acting as an instant survey, generating instant and useable data, even though there will be a significant margin of inaccuracy and key areas of omission. This in itself may give rise to discussion. If, for example, it is discovered that the group has a tendency to minimise the real hours spent in front of a screen, what does this tell us about the way these media are perceived?

The exercise will also tend to generate both average and unusual results. This, in turn, may lead to valuable discussion starters:

> Leader: Angelica seems to get a lot of her information from the Internet, whereas in Jamal's house information is received through television and newspapers only. Which media are likely to give accurate information? Which a range of opinions? Does the quantity of TV channels effect the quality of the information? If so, how?

Follow-on sequence

The ritual of 'Arrange yourself..' is slightly adapted to become 'quick lists' – a brainstorming game. The speed required to win is used to explore instant responses, the things at the front of the players' minds.

The teams are now given a group task to complete to explore the topic of media representation. Write down a list of ten in each of the following categories. The first team to finish and sit back down in a line gains the point.

Writers
Musicians
Sports people
Politicians

Each group is then asked to look at their instant lists and see if the ten people have anything in common other than the category itself. If the group need prompting, ask them to look at race, gender and disability.

Are there any groups underrepresented in any of the categories? If so, why is that?

The next 'quick list' addresses representation issues more directly:

Write down the name of ten well-known non-fictional people, alive or dead, in each category:

Black and Asian people
Disabled people
Women

Black and Asian People
Gabrielle
Sol Cambell
Gandhi
Nelson Mandela
Will Smith
Wassim Akram
Linford Christie.
Diane Abbott
Meera Syal
Moira Stuart

Then the group reflects on the lists:

• Take a world map. Put a pin in the map to indicate which country you think the person was born in. What do these clusters tell you about who is well-known?

• How many of the people on the lists have political power or influence? How does this compare with the initial 'politicians' list?

• Which lists were easier to think of? Which were harder?

• How many are sports people or entertainers and from which categories?

The exercise is repeated for fictional characters:

Disabled fictional characters
Long John Silver
Scar in the Lion King
Richard III
Al Pacino's character in 'Scent of a Woman'.
The Seven Dwarves
Quasimodo
Tiny Tim in A Christmas Carol
Dustin Hoffman's character in 'Rainman'.
Mike in Brookside
Captain Hook

Which classic story archetypes best fit these characters; hero/heroine, baddy, victim, comic relief etc?

Who is responsible for depicting these characters? What effect does the author, actor or illustrator have on the way society views this group of people?

This exercise leads on to a range of drama and research projects for the group:

For example, to pursue the issue of disability, the group starts to define the term first. The distinction between the 'medical' and 'social' models of disability is proposed. A group brainstorming of associated words is compared to the following quote from David Hevey (1992).

> *Impairment:* Lacking part of or all of a limb, or having a defective limb, organism or mechanism of the body.
>
> *Disability:* The disadvantage or restriction of activity caused by a contemporary social organisation which takes no or little account of people who have physical impairments and thus excludes them from the mainstream of social activities.

The group then considers the status of, say, people with learning disabilities, hidden disabilities such as epilepsy, people who are or have been in the mental health system and people living with HIV. Are these people disabled in the same way as blind people, deaf people and wheelchair users?

The group research the lives of a variety of disabled people and use their evidence as the stimuli for further drama and citizenship work.

Alien alphabet

Alien Alphabet is an exercise that has the advantage of locating individual concerns within a collective endeavour. Its other benefit is that the limitation imposed by the exercise enables the group to set the agenda for future sessions or even a whole programme of work.

Although I have focused mainly on one follow-up sequence to this exercise, Alien Alphabet lends itself to many alternative drama strategies.

Each player writes a 'child's alphabet' on a piece of paper ('A is for..., B is for... etc) designed to teach an alien what is important about the player's community. There's a time limit on the exercise (say 5 minutes) and players are encouraged to find a word for every letter in this time.

A	is for	Aggression
B	is for	Buildings
C	is for	Conflict
D	is for	Darkness
E	is for	Environment
F	is for	Family
G	is for	God
H	is for	Health
I	is for	Illness
J	is for	Judgement
K	is for	Kindness
L	is for	Love
M	is for	Mugging
N	is for	Numbers
O	is for	Ownership
P	is for	Police
Q	is for	Quiet
R	is for	Recreation
S	is for	Shopping
T	is for	Travel
U	is for	Underworld
V	is for	Violence
W	is for	Weekend
X	is for	X-rated
Y	is for	Youth
Z	is for	Zest

Each player then transfers their list, one word at a time, onto twenty-six separate large sheets of paper, one for each letter of the alphabet. Some of the words are likely to be repeated, so players are assured that writing the word out again is useful, as it indicates the importance of this word to the group as a whole. The sheets of paper are placed strategically around the room and the group is given the task of contemplating these lists of words in silence. After a few moments, the players are told to stand next to a sheet of paper that holds a special meaning for them. The leader guides this part of the exercise carefully, encouraging each player to follow their instincts about which words, or combinations of words, are important. It's often worthwhile to prompt a group to bring to mind images that relate to words in combination (for example, what images are brought to mind by pairs of words such as 'health and housing', 'race and religion', 'environment and education' etc). If at all possible, players should try to make independent choices regardless of their friends and peers.

In this way, one small group will cluster around a particular sheet of paper. In a few cases, individuals and pairs may be standing on their own. As the next part of the exercise requires working in small groups, individuals and pairs should be invited to pick up their sheet of paper and join others to create small groups of four to six players.

The small groups will all now have a collection of key words to use as a stimulus for further work.

Follow-on work

There are now many possible alternatives for consolidating the initial phase of this exercise, such as:

- the creation of small scenes showing the relationship between words

- the building of machines using movement and sounds that relate to a chosen word (e.g. 'a money machine', or 'a war machine')

- creating a 'documentary' explaining a key concept to the alien

The next series of tasks demonstrates in greater depth one specific way to focus the session on citizenship.

The leader asks the group to think again about an alien who knows nothing about their community. At the moment, it has an alphabet that explains isolated ideas and concepts in society. We would now like to teach it something about being a citizen in its community.

Each group chooses one word that was popular with the group as a whole and is also important to their small group. The group is asked to create and present two contrasting still images depicting this word. The first image shows a *right being denied*, the second *the taking on of a responsibility*.

The group choose to explore the word 'family'.

A right being denied
The first image is symbolic. It shows a child being physically pulled two ways by competing parents, a grandmother helping the father and a grandfather standing aloof, not getting involved.

The taking on of a responsibility
The second image is naturalistic. It shows a family dinner, with a child helping to feed an elderly relative.

As these images are the first fragments of a narrative, they lend themselves to a range of further drama exercises, reflection and discussion.

A day in the life

This exercise is also adapted from Augusto Boal and is described in *The Rainbow of Desire* (1995). It is a particularly useful way to encourage people who are fearful of or unused to drama to enjoy working in role. It begins as a 'pure' drama exercise, unlocking the imagination in a private way, so it doesn't have any of the presentational elements of theatre. Fears that players might have about being judged on their acting ability are minimised and they can focus on exploring the world 'as if' they were another person.

Each player in the group is given a sealed envelope with a picture inside it. They're under strict instructions not to open the envelope until a signal is given. The group walk around the room as independent spirits, without acknowledging the other players. At the signal, each player finds a space away from others and opens their envelope. Inside is a picture of the character they will become. It's worth noting that the leader could easily just give players their photographs, but the secrecy ritual usefully adds additional tension.

As will become apparent, the nature of the exercise demands that the photographs are carefully chosen to depict a range of diverse characters in a natural setting. If there's a picture of, say, a pop star or a model, it shouldn't be a publicity shot. It may also be useful to choose pictures that relate to a particular theme or issue. For example, the pictures could all show people engaged in their jobs: a nurse, a building worker, a police officer. Indeed, the leader may choose images that deliberately run against stereotype: a male nurse, a female builder, a black police officer. It's mostly wise not to leave the allocation of these roles to chance. The leader should be aware of the potential impact of a role on a particular player. In most cases, it is useful to strike a balance between a role that may challenge prejudices and assumptions (e.g. a particularly macho male as a male nurse) whilst avoiding the potential for public embarrassment and loss of face later in the exercise.

Having reflected on their picture, each player is asked to continue a steady walk around the space while they imagine the daily routine of their character. The leader calls out 'midday' and the players freeze in a depiction of their character at midday on a typical day. The freeze is held for a few seconds and then the characters continue parading around the room. The leader calls out 'one o'clock p.m.' and the characters freeze as if it's an hour later. This process is repeated twenty-four times, for each hour.

It's worth noting that many players will show the character asleep for about eight of the hour images. It can add an extra element not to ignore this and instead encourage players to focus on what's happening while they're asleep. For example, they could depict their characters' dreams or state of mind. This highlights the point that the exercise is designed to enable players to give themselves fully to the process of inhabiting a character. Where appropriate, the leader can coach the group to focus on this authenticity – there's no audience watching and no one to impress; there's no need to be 'dramatic' or 'interesting'. The exercise is concerned with exploring a daily routine as a way to experience being in someone else's shoes.

Once each player has visualised a day in their characters' life, they're asked to choose three contrasting hours from the day to share. This is best achieved in small groups of between four and six players, as sharing in a large group is very time-consuming. In these small groups, each player presents their three images and invites the others to try to work out some key facts about the characters. Then the group is shown the original photographs and they briefly discuss the characters. The leader can add additional focus by asking the group to discuss which aspects of the character are invented by the player and which come directly from the information in the picture.

There are a number of ways the small groups can share their learning with the whole group. For example:

- Each small group presents three still images of all their characters together, showing the variety of activities that occur at three key times (say morning, afternoon and evening). The whole group reflects on what they've seen.

- Each group prepares a character parade, introducing each character as if they were a game show contestant with a few salient facts (e.g. '... this is Brendan and he is a nurse at the General Hospital. He is studying computers in order to change careers').

Follow-on work

As with other exercises, the group now has fragments of narrative to build more drama structures. The first task is usually to narrow down the number of stories, as it's too cumbersome to pursue work in depth on every character. The following progression is merely one suggestion, although there are clearly many alternative ways to proceed with this character exercise.

In the following example, the theme of the session which now becomes explicit is 'the politics of the workplace'.

Each small group starts by choosing one character from the previous sequence. They're invited to choose a character who will face profound conflict in the workplace.

Each group creates an 'emotional map'. Players make still images of other people in the workplace, using stylised gestures and expressions that demonstrate their feelings towards the protagonist.

The protagonist turns to each player in turn and improvises an intense twenty seconds of dialogue. The ritual and rhythm of this exercise maintains attention and interest. These mini-scenes are then shared with the group.

These model scenes can then be replayed in different ways to explore interpersonal dynamics. Other players can take the place of the protagonist, trying out different ways of interacting with colleagues. The audience can offer key words as strategies to guide the protagonist. For example, a woman builder who is facing sexism from her colleagues could try being in turn 'assertive', 'calm', 'angry', 'dismissive' or 'sarcastic'.

Can I have a home?

This exercise explores the area of rights and responsibilities, starting with the issue of homelessness. It combines a 'swapping' game with improvisation, relaxing inhibitions and creating an enjoyable experience.

The same question is posed in different ways by a protagonist in the middle, while the rest of the group are encouraged to make swift responses. This ritual is inherent in the game and frames the improvisation element, thus ensuring that the exercise is inclusive and has a compelling rhythm.

Each player finds an object to symbolise their home. The object should be small and not valuable (e.g. a pencil, scarf, piece of paper). The group forms a large circle, each standing in front of their object. One player volunteers to be 'it' and goes in the middle.

The player in the middle approaches another player in the circle and asks whether they can come into their home. The respondent has to find a creative way to say no.

'Can I come to stay in your house?'

'Sorry, I've got all my relatives staying at the moment and there just isn't any room.'

'Could you put me up just for one night?'

'You've got a nerve asking me, I hardly know you!'

During this dialogue, other players in the circle are permitted to swap homes when the leader shouts 'time to move'. The players can catch the eye of a fellow player across the circle and mutually agree to swap. The player in the middle must try to jump in and inhabit a spare home during the frantic swapping. If they succeed, a new 'homeless' player will have to find a new home.

The player in the middle must always try to keep up dialogue with the others, but direct it at different players around the circle.

The game should maintain high energy and playfulness. If the group seems reticent and needs energising, the leader can add an extra rule and shout 'holiday!' – whereupon everyone has to find a new home. Should the leader want to halt the swapping, another command is introduced – 'Sunday lunch!'. The aim is to balance the swapping with the improvisation.

Follow-on exercises

To explore the issue further, the game can be played within a variety of dramatic frameworks, even adapting the exercise to have 'family' groups in the middle. As the focus of the exercise has by now shifted from the swapping game to improvisation, the leader should use the 'holiday!' and 'Sunday lunch!' commands wisely in order to ensure that the improvisation element is undertaken fairly and sensitively.

The leader can choose the situation to suit the character of their group. Some examples could be:

• A single unemployed person approaching private landlords

• A family approaching the council

• A refugee family approaching a charity through a translator (this could be particularly effective with bilingual young people)

With each situation the players around the circle should try to find inventive and plausible ways to say 'no' to the homeless people in the middle.

During reflection, the leader can move on to universal questions of fundamental rights and responsibilities, using charts and brainstorms:

• Is it a basic right to have a home? Who has responsibility to safeguard that right?

• Which other rights are as basic as the right to a home? Where does responsibility lie in each case?

• Can you place basic rights in any order of importance (e.g. food, clean water, work, safety, education, health, housing)?

The exercise can be adapted for any other basic right. Following background work, the leader can introduce a range of issues, including those affecting the developing world. Dramatic frameworks might include:

• Someone begging for food

• Demanding clean water

• An unemployed person asking for casual work

• Approaching the police after a spate of burglaries

• Parents trying to get a child into a school after multiple expulsions

• Asking for an operation deemed too expensive for the National Health Service.

In each case, the group have found a way of experiencing the barriers people may encounter when claiming basic human rights.

Packing a suitcase

This exercise uses basic mime as its starting point. If effectively done, the lack of concrete props can promote a high level of absorption in the exercise. The physical act of miming and observing others mime stretches the imagination, creating a quality of engagement that generates belief in the emerging fictions.

This exercise can also benefit from the leader working in role. Leaders new to drama may find this a bit daunting, but acting ability is not essential here for productive learning. By making the subtle shift from 'this character is...' to 'I am..', the leader is enhancing the experience by signalling permission to the group to explore the issues playfully in role.

This exercise demonstrates another way to create a fictional framework for further drama exploration, through the character associations of a significant object. This technique can be developed creatively for a range of issues, using an assortment of objects, either real or imagined.

With a flourish, the leader produces a real suitcase as if from nowhere. The suitcase is the only concrete object used. As with other props and objects such as keys, maps and photographs, it's useful for the leader to be aware of the symbolism and resonance of this significant object. It's almost impossible for the suitcase not to trigger a range of story fragments, particularly if it is carefully chosen. A brown leather suitcase with old-fashioned fastenings, for example, might be particularly suitable.

The leader starts the exercise with a familiar scenario – packing for a holiday:

Leader:	We've been offered the chance to go away to the seaside with Auntie Gladys for a few days. As you know, she doesn't have much room in her car, so we can only take one suitcase. What's essential to take?
	'Clothes!'
	'Shoes.'
	'Sponge-bag.'
Leader:	OK, you've got lots of ideas. We'll go round the circle and fill up the suitcase. Just mime the thing you want to take, making sure that you are as accurate as possible about its shape and size. If it comes to your turn and you think the case is full and your object is more important than another, then do a swap. Let's see if we reach a point where the whole group can agree the contents. We'll keep a list on the board just to remind us.

Clearly, the group dynamic will determine whether sufficient consensus can be reached for the exercise to be completed. The leader-in-role can clarify key points as they arise, in terms of what is available at the holiday home (sheets, towels etc). If the group cannot resolve disputes satisfactorily, this itself should be viewed as an interesting starting point for discussion, rather than a failure.

The reflection explores the concept of need:

*   Is there anything essential we couldn't fit in?

*   Do different people have different needs? Are there gender differences? What about the needs of disabled people?

*   What's the difference between a 'need' and a 'want'?

Follow-on exercises

As 'packing a suitcase' has now entered the group's drama vocabulary, the exercise can be used for situations beyond their immediate communal experience.

Some scenarios may be close to the experience of the group, so this could be a good opportunity to validate their experiences. By contrast, some of the situations may need careful handling and the distance of a historical perspective may be wise if the leader senses existing bullying or victimisation might be exacerbated.

In the following exercises, practical research can be brought to life through the drama. The act of packing a suitcase is now only one element of the drama, as the group can explore a range of issues affecting a family who are being forced to move:

• A Kurdish family packing to leave Turkey to stay with an aunt in one room in North London. Who are we leaving behind? How will we stay in contact? What kind of welcome should I expect in England?

• A Jewish family leaving Amsterdam in 1940, based on reading the *Diary* of Anne Frank or studying the paintings of Charlotte Salomon. How has the Nazi invasion changed our lives? What do I know about the concentration camps? Where can we go that is safe? Who can we trust?

• Mother has received threats from a violent ex-partner. She fears for the family's safety – they must leave tonight. Where can we go? Who will offer protection? How could the police and social services help us?

• The family has received an eviction notice from a private landlord. We are heavily in debt and cannot pay the bill. The parents decide to leave immediately, with space in a friend's car for only vital possessions. Where do we go? How did we get into this situation? Who can help?

Schemes of work generated from this exercise also lend themselves to follow-up writing tasks. It's worth noting that writing-in-role (diaries, letters, e-mail correspondence...) and scripting (either from remembered improvisations or video and tape transcription) are strategies which often encourage reluctant writers.

4

One Thursday – a short play

Devised by Danny Braverman, Abigail Amani Chant, Antonia Coker, Natasha Cox, Deni Francis, Keith Saha, Julia Samuels For Theatre Royal Stratford East

Scene A – Shaheen I

Shaheen's home. Still image: **Dad** *reading the paper*

Enter **Shaheen**

Shaheen: [*To audience.*] Eight fifteen. Shaheen at breakfast.

The scene comes to life. Shaheen starts to eats her cereal standing up.

Shaheen: Dad, have you got my dinner money?

Dad: It's on the table, love.

Shaheen: There's only one pound fifty here.

Dad: That's how much your dinner costs, isn't it?

Shaheen: Yeah, but I've got dance tonight. I need twenty p subs.

Dad: What happened to the five pound that I give you on Friday?

Shaheen: Yeah, but I went to the pictures with Tanya, I spent it.

Dad: Well you should have thought on and saved some of it, love. I'm sorry.

Shaheen: Dad! It's only twenty p. Go on... have a look in your pockets.

Dad: Listen, I've got twenty pound to last us...

Shaheen: But...

Dad: ...for the next two weeks.

Shaheen: ... but Dad!

Dad: That's got to go on housekeeping... on leccy... and rent. It's already spent love. I'm sorry.

Shaheen:	But twenty pounds is loads of money.
Dad:	It's nothing.
Shaheen:	Dad, look in your pockets, I heard you jingle. Bet you've got a pound in there or something.
Dad:	Go on... have a look in the pennies jar if you're that desperate.

Shaheen *goes to look in jar.*

Shaheen:	[*Counting.*] There's fifty... sixty... seventy... seventy-four p here Dad.

Shaheen *looks at* **Dad** *as if to say 'can I have it?'*

Dad:	Go on then.
Shaheen:	Yeah, Dad, right. but the thing is, it's not quite enough. Yeah... let me explain right. Coz it's twenty p subs... forty p bus there... forty p bus back... that's a pound already yeah? And then I need drink after dance coz I get really dehydrated.
Dad:	Well, I'll pick you up in the van, love.
Shaheen:	No Dad. Don't do that.
Dad:	Why not?
Shaheen:	I'm not being funny or anything, but it's shameful.
Dad:	Are you saying you're ashamed of your own father?
Shaheen:	No, not of you... nah... nah... it's just like... the van.
Dad:	There's nothing wrong with that van.
Shaheen:	Dad it's all mashed up, there's those horrible big ladders on top of it......
Dad:	Well if you're that.... if you're that ashamed of me, I'll pick you up round the corner then.
Shaheen:	Just give me the bus fare....
Dad:	Give us a ring when you want picking up.
Shaheen:	[*Storming out.*] Whatever!
Dad:	Eh, what about your breakfast?

Dad *freezes. A beat.*

Scene B – Mikey 1

Mikey's flat. Still image: **Jimmy** *on the sofa watching TV,* **Mary** *sitting on a separate chair.*

Enter **Mikey**

Mikey: [*To audience.*] Eight-thirty. Mikey at breakfast.

The scene comes to life.

Mikey:	'Ere sit up, Jimmy mate.
Jimmy:	You watchin' Pokemon?
Mikey:	Yeah! Yer got a problem wiv that?
Jimmy:	Nah, man. It's nang!

They mess about making a racket.

Mary:	[*Walking across them to the post.*] Will you two keep the noise down.
Mikey:	[*Singing.*] Gotta catch 'em all!
Both:	[*Singing.*] Pokémon.
Jimmy:	Mum! I can't see!
Mary:	And I can't hear meself think.
Mikey:	And what were you doin' playin' Crash Bandicoot til all hours?
Jimmy:	Shush!
Mary:	Jimmy, what've told you about playing Playstation in the middle of the night?
Jimmy:	You grassed me up!
Mikey:	Sorry mate.
Mary:	Can I have a bit of quiet?
Mikey:	What is it anyway?
Mary:	It's a housing form.
Mikey:	What, are we moving house like?
Mary:	Well... that's the idea.
Jimmy:	Does my dad know?
Mary:	Of course he does Jimmy, we sat down and talked about it.
Mikey:	Does that mean I can have me own bedroom?

Mary: Well that was always the plan, Mikey, remember.

Mikey and **Jimmy** glare at each other.

Mikey: I'm gonna have the bigger bedroom, I'm older.

Mary: Come on, give me a hand instead of larking about with Jimmy. Now we've got to choose an area to move to. We've got to choose out of these....E6... E7... E13... E21....

Mikey: E21!!! Mum, don't move us there, it's well rough. He'll get his head kicked in in five minutes.

Jimmy: Shut up.

Mikey: You would though.

Jimmy: No!

Mary: We could put down E21. The letter says we'll get moved more quickly if we choose 'less desirable areas'.

Mikey: So how long's it going to take then? Couple of months?

Mary: Longer than I thought, that's for sure. Maybe three years.

Mikey: [In disbelief.] Three years?

Mary: That's what I thought. We can request a garden... but... can't be too fussy I suppose. I'll talk to Ron about it.

Mikey: Whatever.

Mary: Jimmy, have you got your stuff ready for school?

Jimmy: Yeah.

Mary: Mikey?

Mikey: Yeah, I'm not goin' to forget my homework today, am I? I'm handing in Urban Legend.

Jimmy: Yeah, Mikey's art's wicked! Show it her.

Mary: What?

Mikey: Nah.

Mary: Go on then. Be quick.

Mikey: OK. But it's, like, on a really big scale.

Mikey starts to get out his art piece. It's very big, lots of pieces of A2 paper carefully stuck together.

Jimmy: And Spanner's gonna have it on his new CD as the cover.

Mikey: You hold it up there, Jimmy.

Mary:	Whose Spanner?
Mikey:	Yeah. Spanner. Nigel's new name, innit? MC Spanner.

Jimmy *stands on a chair and puts his foot through the picture.*

Mikey:	What've you done?
Jimmy:	I didn't mean....
Mikey:	You stupid little git! I'll... I'll.......get off it.
Jimmy:	Sorry... I'll... I'll...

Jimmy *tries to fix it and makes it worse.*

Mary:	Leave it Jimmy!
Mikey:	You've made it worse! Do you know how long it took me to make this?
Jimmy:	It was an accident! I'll mend it.
Mikey:	Just shut up! You're not wanted!

Jimmy *starts to cry and leaves the room.*

Mary:	Now look what you've done! Jimmy love!
Mikey:	Jimmy love! I've failed! I've failed me GCSE!
Mary:	Can't it be mended?
Mikey:	I can't... it's ruined!
Mary:	It's only a drawing! Little Jimmy could do that!
Mikey:	Only a drawing... It's got to be in today. Did you notice the detail on that? Its has to be in tomorrow.
Mary:	Say sorry to Jimmy.
Mikey:	You what?
Mary:	Say sorry to Jimmy. You agreed....
Mikey:	What?
Mary:	He's crying his eyes out because of you. You agreed to make the best of this situation.
Mikey:	I didn't agree to having my whole life ruined when your boyfriend...
Mary:	He's got a name...
Mikey:	...when Ron and Jimmy moved in. I won't get into art college now, mum – don't you understand?

Mary:	You've got til the end of the day to get it done haven't you?
Mikey:	Yeah.... but it took me...
Mary:	So don't stress me out. Take responsibility Mikey. The longer you argue...
Mikey:	Yeah, you're right. I'm off.

Mikey *goes in a huff, throwing the art work in her face.*

| **Mary**: | Mikey! What about Jimmy? You're supposed to take Jimmy to school. (*Shouting*) You're selfish Mikey! Just plain bloody selfish! |

Freeze. A beat.

Scene C – Shaheen 2

The Playground. Still image: **Tanya** *looking tired.*

Enter **Shaheen**

Shaheen: [*To Audience.*] Twelve forty-five. Shaheen at lunch.

The scene comes to life.

Shaheen: Come on Tanya, you're so slow today.

Tanya: I'm so tired, Shaheen. It's that paper round I'm doing. I have to get up at six-thirty every morning.

Shaheen: Six-thirty!!

Tanya: ...and then I work seven days a week and I only get eight pounds.

Shaheen: Eight pounds!

Tanya: It's no good man, it's well out of order.

Shaheen: But eight pounds is eight pounds!

Tanya: But it's not enough is it? Seven days a week.

Shaheen: Yeah, well even so....it's better than nothing.

Tanya: I'm thinking of giving it up anyway. Oh come on Shaheen, let's go to the chicken shop and have some lunch.

Shaheen: I'm not really very hungry.

Tanya: Oh come on Shaheen.

Shaheen: I've got crisps and stuff in my bag, Tanya, yeah.

Tanya: Crisps ain't going to fill you up.

Shaheen: Yeah, but I had a big breakfast, alright.

Tanya: Oh Shaheen, just come in there with me please.

Shaheen: Just coz you're hungry for the guy in the chicken shop.

Tanya: No! He's well butters!

Shaheen *and* **Tanya** *laugh as the scene changes to become the Chicken Shop. The Chicken Shop Man is behind the counter.*

Chicken Shop Man: Hello, can I help you please?

Tanya: Can I have two pieces of chicken, some chips.... and a coleslaw and a large Fanta.

Chicken Shop Man: Large Fanta.

As he turns around to get the food **Shaheen** *and* **Tanya** *giggle.*

Tanya: Woah, Look at him!

Shaheen: [*Giggling.*] I bet when he turns round he smiles at you... you watch.

Chicken Shop Man: [*Giving* **Tanya** *the food.*] That's two pounds forty-nine please, darlin'.

Chicken Shop Man *gives* **Shaheen** *a slow wink and a smile. The girls crack up laughing. They exit.*

Chicken Shop Man: See ya!

Tanya: Yeah. [*Giggles.*]

The scene changes to the pavement outside the shop.

Shaheen: Tanya, are you going dance tonight?

Tanya: Yeah I'll meet you at the bus stop, and we'll get the bus together.

Shaheen: No, no, I was thinking we could walk – a sort of pre-warm-up-warm-up.

Tanya: But Shaheen I've just told you, I'm really tired....

Shaheen: ...but...but...

Tanya: Let's just get the bus yeah.

Shaheen: Alright.

Tanya *gives one chip to* **Shaheen.** *A chip – not a chicken leg!*

They freeze. A beat.

Scene D – Mikey 2

The Artroom. Still image: **Ms Askew** *arranging a display.*

Enter **Mikey**.

Mikey: [*To audience.*] Three-forty. Mikey sees his art teacher after school.

The scene comes to life. **Mikey** *knocks at the door.*

Ms Askew: Yep, come in!

Mikey: Alright miss, how's it going?

Ms Askew: Yeah, hi Mikey, hi. What do you think of this new Monet?

Mikey: It's not really my scene to tell you the truth, miss.

Ms Askew: [*Ignoring him.*] Mmm.... I've put it opposite the door – it's got a really good calming effect....

Mikey: I really need to speak to you, miss?

Ms Askew: Now? Can't you make an appointment?

Mikey: It has to be now, miss.

Ms Askew: I've got a meeting with the Head of Year in two minutes. I'll tell you what, I can give you a minute and a half. So, what's your problem?

Mikey: The thing is... I've been having a few problems. You know my final piece has got to be in tomorrow....

Ms Askew: ... at the beginning of the school day... yes.

Mikey: The thing is... it got ruined. It's a long story... but...

Ms Askew: [*Sighing.*] So what are you going to do if, as you say, it's 'ruined'. Sure you're just not being a bit dramatic?

Mikey: It is ruined... my mum's boyfriend's son...

Ms Askew: Mikey, I haven't got time to hear your family history. You know I can't give you an extension. It's out of my hands. The external examiner....

Mikey: It's not that I've neglected it. It's unfair, miss. Look at the preparatory work.

Ms Askew: [*Looking at a piece of work.*] Yes, you have really put a lot of work into it. I can see that you really....

Mikey *takes the drawing* **Ms Askew** *is holding and turns it the other way up.*

Ms Askew:	Right, oh, right, yes, no, no, I can see where you're going with this now Mikey. It's got like a street feel?
Mikey:	Yeah. It's called Urban Legend.
Ms Askew:	Urban. Yes....
Mikey:	So can I have at least till Monday then?
Ms Askew:	No. But just tell me how you could redo it by tomorrow morning. [*She looks at her watch.*]
Mikey:	What if I sprayed the side of the school wall, can I ....
Ms Askew:	No.
Mikey:	It needs to be big scale.
Ms Askew:	Yes, big .... You want a really big size piece to make an impact in your portfolio. Now... [*She picks up a huge piece of hardboard.*] What about this?
Mikey:	Not big enough.
Ms Askew:	It'll have to be. You could do your hippity-hop thing on this.
Mikey:	Hip-hop, miss.
Ms Askew:	Yeah.... hip-hop.... yeah.
Mikey:	Sorted then. [*Moving towards the kettle.*] Miss....and me cans from the locker.
Ms Askew:	Oh Mikey, you can't use the art room, not tonight.
Mikey:	Why not?
Ms Askew:	I'm sorry, I've got to rush to my meeting....
Mikey:	I thought that's what you meant, miss.
Ms Askew:	No, I can't supervise you tonight....
Mikey:	I'm not being funny or anything miss, but I haven't got anywhere else to do it....
Ms Askew:	Well you're going to have to do it at home.
Mikey:	I don't think that'll be possible miss, you know.... This was the only place to do it in the first place.
Ms Askew:	Not an option. Look, I'm sorry, I'm afraid I can't think of anything else. I mean, why not the street? That's where the art originated from after all....
Mikey:	It's pouring with rain, miss.... Your board will get all soggy.

Ms Askew: [*No longer listening. Looking at her watch.*] Listen Mikey, to be honest, if you really cared about this you'd have looked after it properly and wouldn't be in this position.

Mikey: It's not my fault!

Ms Askew: It never is, is it?

Mikey: I can't do it at home! There's just no room. My mum won't let me.

Ms Askew: Mikey, try solutions not problems. Other students manage it.

Mikey: Yeah, but they don't....

Ms Askew: Look at Darren Carr for instance.

Mikey: Darren....

Ms Askew: It would surprise you to learn what other people overcome if they have to. Right... out now...

Mikey: But...

Ms Askew: [*As she shows him out.*] And I expect you to pull your finger out and have that in first thing tomorrow morning.

They freeze. A beat

Scene E – Femi 1

Split action – Femi's living room and a nearby children's playground. Still image:
Paul *sits on a climbing frame.*

Enter **Femi**

Femi: [*To audience.*] Four-thirty, Femi at home.

Femi *sits down to watch TV. On the other side of the stage, his mate* **Paul** *makes a phone call.* **Femi**'*s mobile phone rings. He picks it up.*

Femi: Wha' blo'?!

Paul: Whaasssuup?

Femi: Whaasssuup?

Paul: You alright?

Femi: Yeah mate.

Paul: Listen yeah, I'm in the playground outside your house. Look out your window.

They both look directly ahead. By their responses we can tell that they can see each other. They laugh and wave.

Paul: You coming out, yeah?

Femi: I dunno man, I've got to do my homework.

Paul: What's that about, man? Sack it, yeah?

Femi: No man.

Paul: Do it on the bus in the morning, innit?

Femi: Alright let me ask my mum, yeah. [*To Sola*] Mum! Mum!

Sola: [*Entering.*] What is it Femi? I'm trying to....

Femi: [*Covering the phone.*] Mum, can I go out with Paul please?

Sola: Paul? Paul Smith?

Femi: Yeah.

Sola: What have I told you about that Paul Smith?

Femi: But...

Sola: You know I don't like you hanging around with him....

Femi: But he's alright... there's nothing wrong with him.

Sola: [*Noticing him out of the window.*] Look at him sitting on that kids' playground. He's going to break it.

Paul *notices her and waves. She waves back with a fixed grin.*

Femi: Go on mum, for half an hour, please.

Sola:	Half an hour Femi...
Femi:	Sweet....
Sola:	I'll you be watching you.
Femi:	Alright. [*To the phone.*] Smithy – soon come yeah.
Paul:	Sweet.

They hang up. **Femi** *leaves his half of the stage and goes over to* **Paul**. *They greet each other.*

Both:	Whaasssuup!
Femi:	[*Posing for him.*] Check out the hat! You're not ready for the hat! Check out the crepes!
Paul:	That hat is late.

Femi *ignores him and struts around showing off.*

| **Paul**: | Nah, nah... |

Paul *takes the hat and puts it on, mocking* **Femi**. **Femi** *tries to chase him.* **Paul** *continues to wind him up and* **Femi** *joins in the game. They continue to fool around, making more and more noise.*

Femi:	What you doing?
Paul:	Bust me up for it, bust me up!
Femi:	Give me back my tings man!
Paul:	Bust me up for it!
Femi:	That's out of order!

The play fighting continues while **PC Powell** *enters, unseen by the lads.*

| **PC Powell**: | Oi. What's your problem? |

The boys immediately stop what they are doing, and sit on the climbing frame. They look at the ground.

| **PC Powell**: | I know you, don't I? Smith? One of the Smith brothers. [*Pause.*] I don't know your little friend. [*Pause. To* **Femi**] I'd watch the company I keep if I was you. [*Pause.*] I'll be keeping a close eye on the pair of you lads. [*He exits.*] |

Paul *takes the hat off and gives it to* **Femi**.

Femi:	[*Kisses teeth.*]
Paul:	Didn't do nothing.
Femi:	How comes they know your name.
Paul:	My brothers, innit.

Femi: They was in trouble a long time ago.

Paul: You know what I'm saying.

Femi: Where we supposed to go anyway? Well out of order.

Pause. **Femi** *shoves the hat in his pocket.*

Femi: I'm going home now.

Paul: What you going in for? Just because of that?

Femi: No man, I just wanna go inside, you know what I mean?

Paul: Why? But I didn't do nothing.

Femi: I know that Smithy man, but I've got to go and do my homework. Later, yeah.

Paul: Later.

Femi *shakes* **Pauls**' *hand. Freeze.*

Scene F – Mikey 3

Mikey's *bedroom. Still image:* **Jimmy** *is on his bed playing Playstation.*

Enter Mikey.

Mikey: [*To audience.*] Five-thirty. Mikey in his bedroom.

The scene comes to life.

Mikey *comes into the room with the board and his portfolio. It is a very cramped space.*

Jimmy:	Oi! What do you think you're doing?
Mikey:	Can you hold that a second please Jimmy, mate? [*He shoves the board at* **Jimmy**]
Mikey:	Just hold that one second.
Jimmy:	[*Squealing from behind the board.*] Stop it! Does your mum know you've got that here?
Mikey:	No, and I don't want her to know, so shut up.
Jimmy:	Mikey there's no room up here, man.
Mikey:	Hold it for one second and I'll make some room.
Jimmy:	Can't you put it on your side?
Mikey:	I will.

Mikey *moves his bed into the middle of the room to create more space.*

Jimmy:	This ain't fair, man!

Mikey *snatches the board from* **Jimmy**.

Jimmy:	Get off!

Mikey *leans the board against the back wall of the room. He takes out his preparatory work.*

Jimmy:	What you doing anyway?
Mikey:	I'm re-doing my art project because some chief ripped it.

Jimmy *picks up preparatory sheet and looks at it.* **Mikey** *turns the sheet around, so it's the right way up.*

Jimmy:	[*Dropping the drawing on the floor.*] This is crap, man!
Mikey:	You liked it this morning!
Jimmy:	Yeah, well, anyone can draw.

Jimmy *goes back to the Playstation.* **Mikey** *takes out his spray paints.*

Mikey: Come on, open the window will you?

Jimmy: No, I'm cold.

Mikey: Open the window!

Jimmy: No!

Mikey: Open the window.

Jimmy: No.   [*Pulls a face.*]

Mikey *jumps up as if to hit* **Jimmy**. **Jimmy** *scampers up, opens the window and sits down at the Playstation sulking.* **Mikey** *sprays some paint on the board.* **Jimmy** *coughs.* **Mikey** *looks at him meaningfully, shushes him and sprays again.* **Jimmy** *coughs again louder.* **Mikey** *glares at him and sprays again.* **Jimmy** *coughs very very loudly.*

Jimmy: [*Still coughing.*] Mary! Mary!

Mikey *jumps up and covers* **Jimmy's** *mouth to stop him calling out.*

Mikey: Shut up! Shut up...

Mary *enters.*

Mary: Mikey! Get off him!

Mikey *lets go of* **Jimmy**, *who coughs some more.*

Mary: Jimmy, love, are you OK?

Jimmy *is trying to get his breath back and points accusingly at* **Mikey**.

Mikey: Mum, I never meant to....

Mary: What do you think you were doing? You know he's got
             asthma.

Jimmy: [*Still pointing at* **Mikey** *through his wheezes.*] He's bullying me,
             Mary.

Mikey: Jimmy, I'm sorry mate, I forgot you had asthma.

Mary: Jimmy, go and get a glass of water.

Jimmy exits.

Mary: Mikey, what is wrong with you? Have you gone mad?

Mikey: Mum, I'm sorry.

Mary notices the board behind Mikey.

Mary: Mikey!

Mikey *turns to the board and starts to explain.*

Mikey:	I had nowhere else to do it, Mum.
Mary:	Well do it at school.
Mikey:	I can't. They won't let me.
Mary:	What's that school like?
Mikey:	It's crap. You sent me there.
Mary:	You watch your mouth. And you can't do that graffiti stuff in here.
Mikey:	Why not?
Mary:	Why not? What have I told you about those cans?
Mikey:	[*Pause.*] I'm not allowed them in the house.
Mary:	And why's that, Michael?
Mikey:	[*Sullenly.*] I don't know... coz of the smell or something....
Mary:	Yes... the smell ... the mess... Jimmy's asthma.
Mikey:	[*Sarcastically.*] Jimmy's asthma!
Mary:	You know, you shouldn't be so selfish. Why don't you think of someone else for a change.
Mikey:	How can you say that?
Mary:	Think a bit about Jimmy? How many times!
Mikey:	...and what about having him and his dad moving into my home? Him keeping me awake at night. [*He indicates the board.*] C'mon mum, this has to be in tomorrow.
Mary:	You're not giving this a chance to work, you know. You promised to get on with Jimmy and Ron... for my sake.
Mikey:	Yeah right. [*Looks back at the board.*] Do you want me to go to college?
Mary:	Yes, if you get a trade. But not to mess about with this nonsense, Mikey. [*Grabbing the board and shoving it at* **Mikey**.] I want this out of here and I want it out now!

They freeze. A beat.

Scene G – Shaheen 3

The Youth Club. Still image: **Tanya** *limbering up.*

Enter **Shaheen**.

Shaheen: [*To audience.*] Six-thirty. Shaheen at her dance class.

The scene comes to life. **Shaheen** *and* **Tanya** *warming up.*

Shaheen/Tanya: Eighteen, nineteen, twenty....[*They star jump. Then stop.*]

Shaheen: Tanya, make sure you stretch your hamstrings properly, yeah. Last time my legs really hurt me the next day, you know.

Tanya: I know what you mean, you know. That step Troy gave us mashed up my back....

Troy *enters.*

Troy: Alright girls, how's it going?

Shaheen/Tanya: [*Still stretching.*] Hi Troy!

Troy: Alright, now everyone who wasn't here last week listen up. Everyone else, get on with the Cisqo routine.

Shaheen *and* **Tanya** *stop and listen to* **Troy**.

Troy: Listen girls, got a bit of bad news.... don't know how to tell you this. Our funding's been cut for the next twelve months.

Shaheen: What?

Tanya: What about our show?

Shaheen: But... that's not fair!

Troy: Shh.... the show is still going ahead. [*Pointedly.*] We had a meeting with the girls last week who happened to turn up. Basically we agreed that for the class to continue the subs would have to go up from twenty pence to two pound.

Shaheen: Two pound!!!

Tanya *starts to giggle.*

Troy: Two.... now is that a problem for anyone?

Shaheen: Two pounds!

Troy: Two pound. C'mon Shaheen, seeing you can afford your mobile phone, I don't see how that can be a problem....cigarettes, Tanya!

[**Tanya** *stops giggling.*]

Tanya: [*Giving him the money.*] Here you go Troy.

Troy: Shaheen?

Shaheen: Yeah.... thing is though right.... like my Dad yeah, this morning he didn't have no change. He's got like a twenty pound note....

Troy: Right....

Shaheen: But, like I've got a pound on me...

Troy: I'll tell you what, as a favour, give us a pound now. Three pounds next week.

Shaheen: Alright then, yeah.

Troy: You sure that's alright?

Shaheen: Yeah... no.... no... it's no problem.

Shaheen *hands over a pound.*

Troy: Thanks.

Tanya: You ready now?

Shaheen: Nah!

All freeze. A beat.

Scene H – Femi 2

Femi's living room. Still image: **Femi** *in front of the TV.*

Femi *comes to life and speaks to the audience.*

Femi: Seven o'clock. Femi back at home.

Femi *goes back into the scene, watching TV.* **Sola** *enters and turns off the TV.*

Femi: Oh what did you do that for, man? I was watching that, Mum.

Sola: Yeah you were watching it.

Femi: What's wrong? What have I done now?

Pause.

Femi: What's the matter, man?

Sola *looks at him and then looks out of the window. She then looks back at* **Femi** *and waits for an explanation.*

Femi: [*Realising.*] Oh, look yeah, I can explain. Yeah, right, we were just sitting there, the policeman just walked....

Sola: Minding your own business?

Femi: Yeah, yeah, right, he just came up, we weren't....

Sola: [*Interrupting.*] Yes I believe you, Femi.

Femi *stops his explanation abruptly.*

Sola: I believe you. You see, this is exactly what I'm trying to tell you ......

Femi: What?

Sola: I don't want you hanging around with that Paul Smith.

Femi: Paul Smith's my bredren man, you can't do that.

Sola: Your bre....what?...Well you'll just have to find a new brethren then.

Femi: You can't stop me from seeing my friends, man.

Sola: What about Darren Carr?

Femi: Darren....

Sola: Why don't you hang out with him?

Femi: You can't stop me from seeing my friends. That's not right, man.

Sola: Yes I can, I'm your mother.

Femi: You can't! You can't....

Sola: I don't want you seeing that Paul Smith and that is final!

Femi *and* **Sola** *freeze. A beat.*

Scene I – Mikey 4

Split action – **Mikey** *in the street and* **Tanya** *and* **Shaheen** *at their dance class.*

Mikey *addresses the audience.*

Mikey: Eight o'clock. Mikey phones his girlfriend Tanya.

The scene comes to life. **Mikey** *gets out his mobile phone and* **Shaheen** *and* **Tanya** *are practising dance steps.*

Tanya: [*Demonstrating a step.*] O.K Shaheen, yeah, Troy says the movement's like this...

Shaheen: Okay, I nearly got it. Do it again.

Tanya*'s mobile phone rings. It plays the Love Story theme.*

Shaheen: Shame Tanya, is that your phone ring? You've got to change that ring you know Tanya!

Tanya *takes the call with a smile. Throughout the conversation,* **Shaheen** *continues with stretches, listening in.*

Tanya: You alright, Mikey?

Mikey: You alright? How's it going?

Tanya: How comes you haven't called me all week?

Mikey: Yeah, I'm sorry about that. I've just been snowed under with all my GCSEs and all that. Did you not get my text messages?

Tanya: Text messages. You're so cheap, Mikey!

Mikey: Listen, I was wondering if I could ask you a really big favour?

Tanya: What's that?

Mikey: ...don't suppose I ....um... stop at yours tonight?

Tanya: [*Grinning.*] That's alright... yeah.

Mikey: Is your Dad in?

Tanya: You know he's out on Thursday night, man.

Mikey: Aaah, nice one, you saved my life. My Ma's just been giving me grief.

Tanya: What about?

Mikey: I don't know. She won't let me do my art project in my bedroom.

Tanya: What are you going to do?

Mikey:	Well, I was thinking like... it'll only take us about an hour or something...
Tanya:	Right....
Mikey:	So, what I was wondering is if I bring it round to yours?
Tanya:	[*Affronted.*] Oh so that's why you're calling!
Mikey:	No....
Tanya:	That's exactly what Shaheen said, you're just using me, man!

Shaheen *gives* **Tanya** *a look.*

Mikey:	No, no....what's Shaheen been saying?
Tanya:	Listen Mikey right, if you want to see me, you can call me after dance, but don't bring that homework round with you, right? [*A beat.*] Right?
Mikey:	Right.

Tanya *ends the call, looks at* **Shaheen**. *Freeze. A beat.*

Scene J – Shaheen 4

The Youth Club. Still image: **Tanya** *and* **Shaheen** *exhausted.*

Shaheen *addresses the audience.*

Shaheen: Eight-thirty. Shaheen at the end of her dance class.

The scene comes to life.

Shaheen: I'm so tired Tanya, you know. Troy makes us work so hard you know.

Tanya: I know, my legs are killing me. Let's go to the chicken shop and get a can of drink.

Shaheen: D'ya know Tanya, I'm really tired. I'm just going to get the bus and go home, yeah.

Tanya: Come on, Shaheen. Look, we weren't there last week, we'll miss out on all the gossip.

Shaheen: Yeah, but I'm really tired.

Tanya: Come on Shaheen, you my friend or not?

Shaheen: Yeah. [*Looking at her money.*] Alright, I've got .... forty-four p, lend me one p and I'll get a drink.

Tanya: Yeah. [*Gives it to her.*] But I want it back.

Shaheen: One p, you're so tight Tanya, you know.

Tanya: Oh Shaheen, guess what?

Shaheen: What?

Tanya: Femi's going to be there.

Shaheen: Femi at the chicken shop! Why didn't you say so?

They giggle. Freeze. A beat.

Scene K – Femi 3

Split action – **Femi** *in his living room and* **Paul** *in the playground.*

Femi *addresses the audience.*

Femi: Nine fifteen p.m. Femi gets a call.

The scene comes to life. **Femi** *is watching TV,* **Paul** *on the climbing frame makes a call on his mobile phone.* **Femi**'s *phone rings.*

Femi: Wha' blo', bruv?

Paul: Whaaassuup!

Femi: Smithy man...Whaaassuup!

Paul: You alright?

Femi: Yeah mate.

Paul: I'm outside your house again. Look outside your window.

Femi *looks out. They laugh and wave.*

Femi: Yeah sweet, man, sweet, it's all good. Anyway, guess what? My mum saw that policeman talking to us, y'know.

Paul: You lie.

Femi: Nah, she was mad.

Paul: What did she say?

Femi: About how I can't hang around with you no more, and you're a bad influence. Your brothers 'n' thing.

Paul: But I didn't do nothing.

Femi: I explained that to the woman, man.

Paul: You better tell her, innit.

Femi: I don't know what to do, man.

Paul: Just come out, yeah.

Femi: Alright, she's sleeping right now, yeah. I soon come.

Paul: Soon.

They end the call. **Femi** *goes over to* **Paul**. *They touch hands.*

Femi: Yeah, safe man.

Paul: You alright?! Bes' tell her...

Femi: I tried to tell her, man, but she wouldn't listen to me.

Pause.

Femi:	You know what?
Paul:	What?
Femi:	It's all that policeman's fault, you know.
Paul:	You know what I'm saying?
Femi:	Man, y' know next time he comes round here, yeah, I'm going to tell him about himself.
Paul:	There's nothing you can do, man. I've been getting it for years.

PC Powell *enters, unseen by* **Femi** *and* **Paul**.

Femi:	I'm gonna defend myself.
Paul:	How you gonna defend yourself then? What you gonna do, slice him up?
Femi:	No man, I'm gonna tell him man, he can't talk to me like that!
PC Powell:	OK Smithy, over by the car, go and talk to my friend.

Paul *doesn't move.*

PC Powell:	Now!
Paul:	[*Going.*] Why? What have I done now? I haven't done nothing.
PC Powell:	Move it. [*To* **Femi**, *who is looking at the ground.*] You. Over here, now. Name?
Femi:	What? [*He walks over to* **PC Powell**.] Femi.
PC Powell:	Femi what?
Femi:	Femi Adewole.
PC Powell:	How do you spell that then?
Femi:	A. D. E. W. O. L. E.
PC Powell:	Femi Adewole, right? Address?
Femi:	Marcus Garvey House E21.
PC Powell:	15, Marcus Garvey House E21. Is that those flats over the back there?
Femi:	Yeah.
PC Powell:	And where were you between six and seven this evening?
Femi:	At home, man.
PC Powell:	At Marcus Garvey House?
Femi:	[*Sarcastically.*] Yeah!

PC Powell: Watch it son. Can anyone verify that?

Femi: Yeah... my Mu... [*He breaks off realising what he's said.*]

PC Powell: Right. Mum's name?

Femi: Sola. [*Slowly.*] S. O. L. A.

PC Powell: Is that Adewole as well then?

Femi: Yes.

PC Powell: Were you anywhere near the off licence on Mandela Street this evening?

Femi: What you talking about, man?

PC Powell: You know the one, the off licence on Mandela Street.

Femi: Look, I've lived here all my life, man, there's no off license on Mandela Street.

PC Powell: Are, you trying to be funny?

Femi: [*Angrily.*] I know why you're doing this! I know exactly why you're asking me these questions! I know why you're picking on me!

PC Powell: Right. That's it, we're going down the station.

Femi: What?

PC Powell: I've had enough of this. You've just failed the attitude test. Come on and mind your head.

PC Powell *pushes down* **Femi**'s *head as if getting into a car. They freeze. A beat.*

Scene L – Shaheen 5

Split action – A deserted bus stop and **Shaheen***'s living room. Still image: Dad watching TV.*

Enter **Shaheen***.*

Shaheen: [*To audience.*] Ten o'clock. Shaheen phones her dad for a lift.

The scene comes to life. **Shaheen** *is on her mobile phone waiting for an answer. The phone in the house is ringing, while* **Dad** *watches football on TV.*

Dad: Come on United! C'mon.

Dad *keeps looking over to the phone, and back to the TV uncertain about whether to answer it at this crucial point in the match. Eventually he clicks the answerphone on. As he speaks the answerphone message,* **Dad** *is glued to the match in front of him.* **Shaheen** *gets increasingly panicky as the message goes on.*

Dad: [*As answerphone.*] I'm sorry I'm not in at the moment, but if you'd like to leave your name and your number, I'll get back to you as soon as possible. Alternatively, you can reach me on my mobile on 0797 134 94 66.......

Shaheen: Dad... Dad my money's running out! I've only got thirty seconds....

Shaheen *continues shouting over the rest of the message.*

Dad: [*Still as answerphone.*] ....alternatively you can get me on my pager on 01245 442211. If you want a plastering job, you can contact my partner Michael in 'The Dog' anytime after eight-thirty. No job too big or too small. Please leave your message after the tone. Thank you. Beeeeeeeeep.

Shaheen: Dad... Dad... it's Shaheen, pick up the phone....shit.

Dad *hears her name, reaches for the phone.* **Shaheen** *realises the money has run out.*

Shaheen: Shit!

Dad: Shit! [*He looks at the TV. West Ham are just letting in a goal.*] Shit!

Freeze. A beat.

Scene M – Mikey 5

Tanya's living room. Still image: **Tanya** *watching TV.*

Enter **Mikey**.

Mikey: [*To audience.*] Ten-thirty. Mikey goes round to Tanya's.

The scene comes to life. **Tanya** *watching TV.* **Mikey** *has his portfolio but no board. He knocks at the door. She answers it.*

Tanya: Alright Mikey?

Mikey: Alright.

Tanya: D'ya get your work done?

Mikey: Not exactly.

Tanya: Come in. What happened?

They sit on the sofa.

Mikey: You don't wanna know, Tan.

Tanya: Oh come on babe, tell me what happened.

Mikey: Well I tried to do it at the back of the flats, but all these little kids were coming up to us taking the piss. I was getting it done, and I was nearly finished and it just started pouring with rain and Miss Askey's board just got mashed up.

Tanya: So where is it now?

Mikey: I chucked it in the skip.

Tanya: You threw your coursework in the skip! Mikey!

Mikey: Well, what did you want me to do? You wouldn't let me bring it round here, would you?

Tanya: [*Looking through the portfolio.*] Well, what's in here? You'll just have to enter one of these, innit? This will do.

Mikey: No. That's just preparatory work, Tan.

Tanya: What are you going to do now?

Mikey: I don't know.

Tanya: Well, thank goodness it wasn't something important like maths or English.

Mikey: [*Stares at her.*] I can't believe you just said that. You're just like all the teachers at school, aren't you? Pushing me to do maths or English or Science. I'm not into that, I want to do Art.

Tanya: But Mikey, how you going to get a job as an artist?

Mikey: I already got forty quid off Spanner. It doesn't matter anyway cos I won't be able to go to art college.

Tanya: Look, Mikey, chill out, yeah, cos Richard Blackwood's on now.

Tanya *puts her arm around him, he shrugs her off. Freeze. A beat.*

Scene N – Shaheen 6

Shaheen's *living room.*

Enter **Shaheen**.

Shaheen: [*To audience.*] Eleven o'clock at night. Shaheen finally gets her breakfast.

The scene comes to life. **Shaheen** *is eating her cereal sitting down.* **Dad** *enters and sits down, facing her.*

Shaheen: What?

Dad: Come on then, let's have it.

Shaheen: What?

Dad: Where the bloody hell have you been, Shaheen?

Shaheen: I've just been walking back from dance, Dad.

Dad: You've just been walking back from dance....Well I've just
been driving   round for the past three-quarters of an hour looking
for you.   Worried sick.

Shaheen: Yeah, But it's not my fault is it, yeah? 'Cause I tried to ring you yeah, and like one, my credit ran out and two, your answerphone was on for like a hundred years....

Dad: Are you telling the truth?

Shaheen: Yeah.

Dad: Your money on your phone had run out?

Shaheen: Yeah.

Dad: So why didn't you use a payphone?

Shaheen: I didn't have any money left.

Dad: And you couldn't have borrowed ten pence off someone?

Shaheen: Everyone had gone home.

Dad: So let me get this straight, yeah. You're by yourself, hanging around on the streets at ten thirty at night, with no money.

Shaheen: I wasn't hanging around. It wasn't my fault. If you'd given me the forty pence for the bus....

Dad: Oh! so it's my fault now is it?

Shaheen:	No, but it's not my fault either right, like dance class went from twenty p to two pounds. Can you believe that? I couldn't believe it right, when Troy just said it and....
Dad:	I'm sorry love, you can't go to dance again.
Shaheen:	What?
Dad:	Well for a start if you're going to get me worried sick every evening, worried about how you're going to get home....
Shaheen:	That's not fair! Dad, but...
Dad:	And if you can't afford the two pounds you can't go.
Shaheen:	But dance is the only....
Dad:	Sit down.
Shaheen:	[*She ignores him.*] ...it's the thing I love, you can't stop me....
Dad:	[*Firmly.*] Sit down!

She sits. Pause.

| **Dad:** | If you can't afford it, you can't go, I'm sorry love. |

Shaheen *doesn't respond.*

| **Dad:** | [*Softly.*] Listen, You know if I had the money, I'd give it to you. |

Shaheen *remains silent.*

Dad:	Eh?
Shaheen:	[*Quietly.*] Yeah.
Dad:	Listen, if you really want to do this dance thing, you need to think about what you do with your money, don't you? Make some sacrifices. If you really want to do it.... What things could you do without?

Shaheen *shrugs.*

Dad:	What about your mobile phone?
Shaheen:	You wanted me to have it in the first place.
Dad:	For safety and security. I'm not saying you should give it up, but I don't think you should be gossiping to your friend on your way to school when you're going to see her in 10 minutes, do you? Am I being fair?

Pause.

| **Dad:** | I'm sorry.... |

Shaheen:	I'll just get a job.
Dad:	[*Laughing.*] You get a job! I can't get a bloody job, how're you going to get a job?
Shaheen:	Well Tanya's got one. She does a paper round, yeah. She was saying she doesn't want to do it any more, so I'll take it over and....
Dad:	You're not doing a paper round, love.
Shaheen:	Why not?
Dad:	Well, it's not safe for a start...
Shaheen:	Let's not even go on this safety business, Dad. What's going to happen to me at six o'clock in the....
Dad:	Anything could happen to you at six o'clock in the morning! It's pitch black, a young girl, like you, by herself on this estate...no chance.
Shaheen:	Dad, it's OK Tanya's been....
Dad:	...like you on her own....
Shaheen:	Dad, but you say that I can't go to dance, but you know I love dance, so I say I'll get a job, right, and you say to me no and it's just not fair....
Dad:	OK, I tell you what to do, get someone to do it with you, how's that?
Shaheen:	Do it with me? So, I'd get up at five-thirty, you must be mad, I'd only get four quid....
Dad:	If you can't find someone, I'll get one of your cousins....
Shaheen:	Oh Dad... no... just forget it. It's not fair! I just can't win!

Shaheen *storms out. Freeze. A beat.*

Scene O – Femi 4

Femi's living room. Still image: **Femi** *with his head in his hands.*

Femi *looks up and addresses the audience.*

Femi:	Two a.m. Femi at home.

The scene comes to life. **Sola** *enters. She goes to the window and looks out. Silence. She walks up to him.*

Sola:	So, satisfied now Femi?

Silence.

Sola:	Got anything to say for yourself?
Femi:	[*Lifts his head up.*] Mum, I swear to you. They threw us in the cell for nothing , I didn't do nuttin'.
Sola:	Have you got any idea what I've been going through? [*Shouting.*] Have you got any idea? I've been pacing up and down this place. I rang all your friends. I thought you was lying dead in the gutter somewhere. [*Pauses. Calming down a bit.*] Well, I'm not doing this no more, Femi. Not after that.
Femi:	Mum....I....
Sola:	You can either stay here and live here in this house, by my rules, or... or ... you can go and live with your Dad. Whatever... I don't care... but I'm not doing this any more.

Sola *goes over to the window and looks out again.*

Femi:	[*Amazed.*] So, you'd chuck me out?

Sola *makes no response.*

Femi:	Fine!

Femi *storms out, leaving Sola standing alone. Freeze. A beat.*

END

5
Using Play Texts and
Theatre Experiences

The main aim of this chapter is to provide practical ideas for group-leaders using *One Thursday* with young people. Although the text worked well for a cast of three professional actors, its structure lends itself to exploration and production by larger groups of non-professional young people.

In its current form it can be acted by between three and thirteen actors, depending on the doubling conventions used. The original production used 'integrated casting', making a virtue of casting against type. Indeed, when using the play with young actors, the action of depicting someone with totally different experiences from your own provides a distinctive opportunity to empathise – and so help to challenge assumptions and prejudices.

I hope the play will also be used with groups who don't have the time or resources to create a full production. Although the three stories in the play work excellently in combination, they also work well as three separate ten-minute plays. You'll notice that the scenes are labelled to facilitate separating out the three 'sub-plays'. I hope that this fills a gap for teachers and youth workers who may find it difficult to find short, relevant plays for young people to perform.

Other group-leaders may feel that the energy needed to create a full production might detract from their citizenship programme. The thematic activities at the end of this chapter are particularly suited to the use of the play as a stimulus for discussion. Even if there can be no prospect of a public performance, the acting games and exercises in the first part of this chapter will serve a dual function: exploring the issues in the play and developing communication/performance skills.

In addition, I hope the ideas and strategies that follow will be freely adapted for use with other plays, using texts and visits to live performances. A local producing theatre or touring company will frequently have a history of presenting shows that directly or obliquely reflect the experiences of their local community and can therefore make a powerful impact on young people. The Theatre Royal Stratford East, where I developed much of the work in this book, has mounted a great number of productions in its history that could be used creatively to explore citizenship. For example, Shelagh Delaney's 'Taste of Honey', Theatre Workshop's 'Oh What a Lovely War' and Brendan Behan's 'The Hostage' are well-known, accessible and enjoyable plays from the theatre's history. More recent examples, available in print at the time of writing, and significantly by Black British authors, are Roy Williams' 'No Boys Cricket Club' and Tunde Ikoli's 'Scrape Off the Black'.

Although devastated by cuts in the past twenty years, there are still a number of Theatre-in-Education (TIE) companies in the UK, working in both the formal and informal sector. Often these companies will offer the most thoughtful, cost effective and stimulating approaches to citizenship.

By collaborating with local theatre producers, educators can discover productions and texts to open up an exciting range of issues. It wouldn't be too far-fetched to suggest that publicly-funded theatre producers may start to feel the need to produce more affordable and relevant work to answer the demand from the education sector. As citizenship education becomes increasingly important, a subsidised theatre that targets mainly higher-income, older adults will lose a valuable audience and renege on its responsibility to reach all members of its community.

There may also be 'classic' plays, particularly if imaginatively produced, that could be an effective catalyst for citizenship education. Examples might include most produced work by Ibsen, Brecht and, of course, Shakespeare. Popular contemporary playwrights such as Arthur Miller, Jonathan Harvey, Timberlake Wertenbaker, August Wilson, Caryl Churchill, Dario Fo and Harold Pinter (particularly in his later plays) are some of the many powerful voices exploring politics and society.

In the case of *One Thursday*, the text is a mostly accurate record of the words and actions of the second production. I hope it will be of practical use to a wide range of young people, who should feel free to adapt the text for their own purposes. The text has been scripted and refined by actors over the course of the first two productions. On each occasion, it was important for the acting team to find ways to make the play fresh and authentic. In practice, this meant encouraging an appropriate level of spontaneous improvisation and embellishment within the parameters of the text. This process of sticking to the spirit of the text, whilst treating it flexibly to achieve the most engaging performance possible, is itself a way of deepening an understanding of the underlying themes. For younger performers, it can be liberating to make small changes to the script; adapting the language to their own geographical and cultural context and changing names and locations to represent their own communities. To start this process, some adaptation exercises are outlined later in this chapter.

Reading the play

It's an alarming thought that the act of reading aloud fills many people with dread. It reminds us of some of the most humiliating and tedious experiences of our formal education. And so, introducing a new text, no matter how well written or relevant, can sometimes seriously inhibit learning. It's therefore essential to find non-threatening strategies to introduce a text to a group.

For this reason, you might want to synthesise the action in the play into its constituent parts and to begin the process with improvisation rather than reading. It's also effective to work gradually towards 'public voice' activity, where the pressure to perform for an audience can create a barrier to exploring meaning.

One Thursday itself works a bit like serial television drama, in that there are multiple story lines that can be separated, even though some of the characters appear in each other's stories. This resemblance to soap opera can be used very effectively, as it will be a familiar form for most young people. The group-leader can bring the play alive by introducing the three protagonists separately and by exploring their narratives prior to a reading of the text.

As preparation for an improvisation, you can prepare short character-by-character scene breakdowns and a sheet containing brief descriptions of the characters in a play. The following 'scene cards' for *One Thursday* are designed to be photocopied, cut up and mounted on index cards.

Scene A: Shaheen 1
Number of characters: 2

Where: Shaheen's flat

Time: 8.15 a.m.

Who: Shaheen, Dad.

What: Shaheen tries to get money for the day.

Dad only has £20 for the next two weeks.

Shaheen bargains to get £2.24.

Key line: Dad: 'It's already spent, love.'

Scene C: Shaheen 2
Number of characters: 3

Where: Outside school

Time: 12.45 p.m.

Who: Shaheen, Tanya, Chicken-shop man.

What: Tanya persuades Shaheen to go to the Chicken-shop for lunch.

Tanya buys her lunch, but Shaheen buys nothing.

Tanya persuades Shaheen to get the bus to their dance class.

Key line: Shaheen: 'I've got crisps and stuff in my bag.'

Scene G: Shaheen 3
Number of characters: 3

Where:	The Youth Club.
Time:	6.30 p.m.
Who:	Shaheen, Tanya, Troy.
What:	Troy tells Shaheen and Tanya that the subs have gone up from 20p to £2.00 for their dance class due to cuts.
	Tanya pays the extra, but Shaheen can only afford a pound.
	Tanya carries on dancing, but Shaheen sulks.
Key line:	Troy: 'I don't see how that can be a problem. Seeing how you can afford your mobile phone.'

Scene J: Shaheen 4
Number of characters: 2

Where:	The Youth Club.
Time:	8.30 p.m.
Who:	Shaheen, Tanya.
What:	Tanya tries to persuade Shaheen to go to the Chicken-shop again to meet some boys.
	Shaheen asks Tanya to lend her one p to afford a drink.
	They go to the Chicken-shop.
Key line:	Tanya: 'You my friend or not?'

Scene L: Shaheen 5

Number of characters: 2

Where:	Bus stop and Shaheen's living room.
Time:	10.00 p.m.
Who:	Shaheen, Dad.
What:	Shaheen phones her dad for a lift home, but the answering machine's on.
	Dad misses the call, as Shaheen's credit runs out on her phone.
Key line:	Shaheen: 'Dad... Dad... it's Shaheen, pick up the phone!'

Scene N: Shaheen 6

Number of characters: 2

Where:	Shaheen's living room.
Time:	11.00 p.m.
Who:	Shaheen, Dad.
What:	Dad tells off Shaheen for walking home alone late at night.
	Shaheen blames Dad for not giving her enough money.
	They try to find a compromise, but Shaheen gets angry and storms off.
Key line:	Dad: 'What things could you do without?'

Scene B: Mikey 1
Number of characters: 3

Where: Mikey's living room.

Time: 8.30 a.m.

Who: Mikey, Jimmy and Mary.

What: Mary has problems filling in a housing transfer form to get a bigger place. (She has recently moved her boyfriend and his son into her house.)

Mikey shows Jimmy and Mary his final large-scale 'street' art piece for his GCSE exam. Jimmy ruins it by accident.

There's an argument. Jimmy leaves in tears and Mikey storms off to school.

Key line: Mary: 'He's crying his eyes out because of you.'

Scene D: Mikey 2
Number of characters: 2

Where: The art room at school.

Time: 3.40 p.m.

Who: Mikey, Ms Askew.

What: Mikey tries to get an extension on his GCSE art project.

Ms Askew refuses.

Mikey gets a polystyrene board to re-do his project.

Key-line: Ms Askew: 'If you really cared about this, you'd have looked after it properly.'

Scene F: Mikey 3
Number of characters: 3

Where:	Mikey (and Jimmy's) bedroom.
Time:	5.30 p.m.
Who:	Mikey, Jimmy and Mary.
What:	Mikey tries to get his art project finished, but Jimmy is in the room playing Playstation.
	Jimmy has an asthma attack when Mikey gets his spray paints working.
	Mary hears the noise and forbids Mikey from doing his art project in the house.
Key line:	Mary: 'Why don't you think of someone else for a change?'

Scene I: Mikey 4
Number of characters: 3

Where:	On the street and at the youth club.
Time:	8.00 p.m.
Who:	Mikey, Tanya, Shaheen.
What:	Mikey phones his girlfriend Tanya on her mobile phone to ask if he can finish his art project at her house.
	Tanya answers the call in the middle of her class and, watched by her friend Shaheen, refuses Mikey.
Key line:	Tanya: 'That's exactly what Shaheen said, you're using me, man!'

Scene M: Mikey 5
Number of characters: 2

Where: Tanya's house.

Time: 10.30 p.m.

Who: Mikey, Tanya.

What: Mikey goes to Tanya's house, having thrown his art project in a skip. (It got ruined by the rain.)

Tanya is unsympathetic. Tired, she settles down with Mikey to watch TV.

Key line: Tanya: 'Thank goodness it wasn't something important like maths or English.'

Scene E: Femi 1
Number of characters: 4

Where: Femi's living room and a nearby children's playground.

Time: 4.30 p.m.

Who: Femi, Paul, PC Powell, Sola.

What: Paul calls Femi on his mobile and persuades him to come out to the nearby playgrond below his flat.

Femi gets permission to go from Sola, his mum.

PC Powell recognises Paul as a member of the notorious Smithfamily and lets the boys know he's about.

Key line: PC Powell: 'I'll be keeping a close eye on the pair of you lads.'

Scene H: Femi 2
Number of characters: 2

Where:	Femi's living room.
Time:	7.00 p.m.
Who:	Femi, Sola.
What:	Sola tells Femi off, having seen him talking to PC Powell from her window.
	Sola forbids Femi from seeing Paul again.
Key line:	Sola: 'I don't want you seeing that Paul Smith and that's final!'

Scene K: Femi 3
Number of characters: 3

Where:	Femi's living room and a nearby children's playground.
Time:	9.15 p.m.
Who:	Femi, Paul, PC Powell.
What:	Paul calls Femi again and persuades him to come out whilst his mum's asleep.
	PC Powell comes down to the playground and questions the boys in connection with a robbery.
	Paul gets taken away on suspicion. Femi is questioned and gets angry with his treatment by the policeman.
	PC Powell takes Femi into the station for questioning.
Key line:	Femi: 'I know why you're picking on me!'

Scene O: Femi 4
Number of characters: 2

Where: Femi's living room.

Time: 2.00 a.m.

Who: Femi, Sola.

What: Femi has been released after spending four hours at the police station.

Sola threatens him with sending him to live with his Dad, if he doesn't abide by her rules in the future.

Femi storms out.

Key line: Femi: 'So, you'd chuck me out?'

Character Descriptions

Shaheen's Story

Shaheen:	15 year-old school girl. Mad about dancing.
Dad:	Her dad. A self-employed builder, currently with no work.
Tanya:	Her best friend. Also mad about dancing and girlfriend of **Mikey**.
Chicken-shop man:	18 year-old who works behind the counter at the local fast-food shop.
Troy:	Youth worker in charge of the dance class.

Mikey's Story

Mikey:	16 year-old. Street artist, currently doing his GCSEs.
Mary:	His mum. Has recently moved her boyfriend Ron and his son Jimmy into their small flat.
Jimmy:	9 year-old. Mary's boyfriend's son. Shares bedroom with **Mikey**.
Miss Askew:	Mikey's art teacher.

Femi's Story

Femi:	15 year-old. Lives on a 'rough' housing estate in London, E21.
Sola:	His mum. Divorced from dad, who lives in Nigeria.
Paul:	15 year-old. Femi's best friend (his 'bredren'). Comes from a family with a 'bad reputation'.
PC Powell:	Beat officer for Femi's area.

The group is divided into small groups containing the correct number of characters. They are given one of the scene cards and the card with the character descriptions for their story. Their task is to prepare an improvisation using only the information provided. For groups unused to this way of working, it can be advantageous to set a time-limit on the exercise. Having read the card a few times and familiarised themselves with the characters, the group arrange chairs and tables to depict the 'where' of the scene. They are prompted for particular details: is there a telephone, TV or games console in the room, for example? Once the 'where' is set up, the group cast the characters and run the scene in real time. The scene will last three minutes and they must try to use the 'key line'. The group-leader announces that there is one minute left. Finally, the group-leader counts down from twenty, encouraging the group to find an ending. If appropriate, scenes are shared, but not if the presentation element might be too exposing for anyone.

The improvised scenes can then be compared to the real text and differences noted. Perhaps there will be words and phrases used in the improvisations that might help with the next exercise – adapting the text.

Adapting the text

As well as creating a sense of ownership amongst a young cast, the process of adaptation can also lead to energetic exchanges about citizenship issues. The following exercises provide some examples and may encourage young people to combine thematic and artistic work.

Adapting the text – Exercise 1

In Scene B/Mikey 1 of *One Thursday*, a fictional area of East London (E21) is described by Mikey as being 'well rough' (page 42).

1. Is there an area like E21 where you live?

2. In what ways is it similar/dissimilar?

3. Can you re-write the play to describe your own area?

Adapting the text – Exercise 2

Create a 'glossary of terms' for the slang/street language used by you and your friends.

1. How is it different to the language used in the play?

2. Do you know where the words come from and their real meanings?

3. Which characters might use which of these words?

4. Can you re-write the play putting in language that realistically depicts your own area?

Adapting the text – Exercise 3

In the course of *One Thursday* the characters refer to their music, food, TV and other contemporary elements. This helps to make the play realistic.

1. Which up-to-date references will an audience of your friends enjoy recognising in the play? (For example, Jimmy and Mikey watch 'Pokemon' on morning TV, Tanya and Shaheen go to the 'Chicken-shop' for fast food. Paul and Femi enjoy acting out the 'wazzup!' advert.)

2. Which references are now dated?

3. Can you think of improvements on these elements for your own audience?

4. Rewrite the play, putting in your own up-to-date elements.

Adapting the text – Exercise 4

1. Try improvising each scene having read it only once. Then read the scene again. Did you invent any lines that you thought were better than the original?

2. Can you re-write the scene to include your own lines?

Adapting the text – Exercise 5

1. How different would the story be if one or more of the characters changed?

2. What if 'Jimmy' was a little girl? What if PC Powell was a black police officer, or a woman? What if Femi was white or Asian? Can you still make Mikey's story interesting if he has to complete a music project?

3. If you like any of these alternatives, try re-writing the play.

Adapting the text – Exercise 6

1. Take one of the main stories and use it as the basis for a longer play, writing new scenes for times when we don't see the characters in the original play.

2. Try writing scenes that show a day in the life of other characters like Tanya, Jimmy and Paul. What barriers and conflicts do they face in the course of the day? Use the format of the 'scene cards' as a way to plan your writing.

Developing a character

The following exercises are based mainly on a naturalistic, or Stanislavskian, approach to developing character (Stanislavski, 1979). As well as supporting rehearsal work towards performance, the exercises can also foster greater understanding of the issues in the play.

Developing character – Exercise 1

The players are each given one of the main characters to study. They make a list of six 'wants' for their characters. They then choose the two most important 'wants', remembering that an actor's job is to interpret a character in their own way and that there is no single interpretation.

Are any of these 'wants' in conflict with each other? Are there any moments in the play when this internal conflict is present? Does the actor personally share any 'wants' with his or her character?

To support players who find this exercise difficult, the following lists can be used by group-leaders. The lists are presented in a deliberately haphazard way to encourage players to choose their own priorities:

Shaheen – Wants

To have enough money to get through the day.

To please her dad.

To stay friends with Tanya.

To keep going to her dance classes.

To be safe.

To have the same things as her friends

Mikey – Wants

To go to art college.

To get on with Jimmy.

To have his own room.

To get his mum's support.

To get support from his teachers.

To get on with his girlfriend, Tanya.

Femi – Wants

To be able to hang about outside without police harassment.

To do his school work well.

To keep friendly with Paul.

To stand up for his rights.

To choose his own friends.

His mum to trust him.

Developing Character – Exercise 2

Look at a favourite scene in more depth. Do any of the characters lie? Do any try to hide their true feelings? When do they say *exactly* what they mean, if at all? What would happen if they said what they wanted to all the time? How would others react?

Developing Character – Exercise 3

Make a list of facts you know about a character. Make another list of facts that are probably true about a character but not explicit in the text (for example, what is Sola's job? Do the main characters go to mixed or single-sex schools?) What difference do these choices make to the way a character is played?

Developing Character – Exercise 4

Choose one of the main characters and mark what other characters say about them. How do they feel about other people's perceptions of them?

These exercises should significantly enhance the quality of acting, and hence the underlying themes and issues of the play. As understanding increases, instincts will invariably take over as part of a rehearsal or workshop process. A group-leader can use the findings from these exercises subtly, avoiding the temptation to demonstrate a 'correct' way to interpret the text. In this way, an unusual outcome often surprises the group, and interesting pace, energy and other performance dynamics will emerge organically.

At moments where players become stuck, the group-leader can help through careful questioning, referring to the character in the first person. At this point it may be worth reminding the group that rehearsals are actually about trying things out – an opportunity to get it wrong rather than having to get it right first time:

> 'You mentioned that it's important for you to 'stand up for your rights' – can you play that section again, bearing that in mind.'
>
> 'You said that you thought you were hiding your true feelings in that line. Experiment with what it's like if the circumstances make it harder for you to hide your feelings, but still say the same line. It doesn't matter if it doesn't work, we can always try something else.'
>
> 'Can you make your entrance again, bearing in mind where you've come from?'

Alternatively, you can encourage players to respond to questioning in role, to focus on a particularly important moment:

'Your best friend has just said 'are you my friend, or not?' How are you feeling?'

'Suspicious.'

'Suspicious of what?'

'Her motives... for wanting to be my friend in the first place.'

'What do you think her motives might be?'

'Someone to boss around.'

'Is this the first time you've felt suspicious about Tanya?'

'Yes... I think it is...'

'Good... let's play that bit again – I think you're clearer on that now.'

Ideas for production

The original tour of *One Thursday* was very simply produced. We limited our use of props to the most minimal, emphasising objects that had particular relevance to the narrative (such as Mikey's board and Femi's hat). We used four ordinary chairs, found in the school hall or youth centre, and these were adapted to become all relevant pieces of furniture. Each actor had one costume, which could be quickly adapted for each of his or her characters. There were many artistic and practical advantages to this straightforward approach to production. For example, the actors' skill in shifting character on stage and moving swiftly between scenes helped considerably to sustain the audience's attentiveness.

For a new production by young people, however, there may well be a range of other production possibilities. For example, slide projection could be used both to enhance the scenes and provide captions at the beginning of each one. A small group project to choose appropriate photographs of familiar locations would not only add to the show itself but would also deepen the group's appreciation of the relevance of the play to their own community.

The original productions also had no music, but music might well add pace and interest to a future production. As with the slide projection, the choosing of a soundtrack could help a group of young people to appreciate the dynamics of the play.

It's also not essential to produce the play 'end on' as we did with the original. In fact, the play's intimacy might well be enhanced by a production with the audience seated on more than one side.

Exploring themes

One Thursday was originally devised as the first element in a Forum Theatre session for young people. It reflected back issues and concerns that had been carefully researched by a team of theatre professionals in East London. Following the performance of the play, the audience was given an opportunity to discuss the issues and to choose which of the three narratives they wanted to look at in more detail.

It was important for us that our audience didn't just look at one issue in isolation but considered the whole world of the play and the interrelationship between the different themes. We worked hard to give the play an authentic feel – so that our audience experienced the emotional journeys of rounded, familiar characters – rather than an animated illustration leading to a limited set of 'correct' interpretations of moral and political questions. For young people, therefore, the storylines themselves – the key dilemmas and feelings of the three protagonists – are the ideal starting points to compare to their own experiences and then to explore universal principles.

If you are using the whole play as a stimulus, it might be useful to begin any thematic work with a brainstorm. Ask the group to write down the issues that were important for them in the play. Our experience of touring the play showed that young people will readily foreground their own concerns. It might be interesting to note whether the overtly 'political' issues such as policing and housing are mentioned in the first instance. By contrast, some groups will instinctively bring to mind the less overtly 'political' issues such as friendship and family. This may tell you something useful about your group's anxieties about citizenship generally.

The following simple activity sheets use drama and discussion exercises to bring the themes in the play to the surface and draw connections between political and personal issues. The starting points for these exercises are the scenarios presented in the play. The discussion exercises use the focus on a fictional world to explore the present reality for the players and encourage lively exchange about broader conceptual and community concerns. The last exercises in the activity sheets are designed to offer the possibility for further action. So, for example, the theme of education in Mikey's story can lead on to concrete suggestions for change within your own school community.

The activity sheets are designed for pair work within a larger group session and to be used in conjunction with the 'scene cards' (page 76). I hope that the activities are flexible enough for group-leaders to select elements with each sheet appropriate to their own circumstances. Players should be encouraged to make notes together for feedback and findings can be charted by group-leaders to kick off large group discussions.

Activity Sheet A

Shaheen's Story

Theme: Money

1. Imagine one of you is Shaheen and one is her Dad. Play their final scene together (Scene N/Shaheen 6) in one of the following different ways to see if their money problems can be solved.

    •   Shaheen compromises as much as possible

    •   Dad offers to take out a loan

    •   They both try to find something to sell

2. Hot-seat each other as the characters (i.e. one of you is the interviewer). Find out how Shaheen and Dad feel about this solution.

3. Can you think of any other ways to play this scenario to help Shaheen and Dad? Try out the most effective and realistic way to improve things.

    Write a summary of Shaheen and Dad's best solution to money problems in the box below.

    ┌───┐
    │   │
    │   │
    │   │
    │   │
    └───┘

4. How does this solution effect Shaheen's other problems:

    •   Her personal safety in a 'rough area'?

    •   Her friendship with Tanya?

    •   Her desire to attend dance classes?

5. If you were Shaheen, what compromises would you make? How important, for example, are mobile phones, designer labels or CDs/video games?

    ┌───┐
    │   │
    │   │
    │   │
    │   │
    └───┘

6. Brainstorm people you both know of who face financial barriers to achieving their personal goals. How severe are these compared to Shaheen's?

7. How do Shaheen's money problems compare to those of people in other parts of Britain or elsewhere in the world?

8. Which of the following items do you think are *necessary* and which are *desirable*? Put your intials in the box that is nearest to your opinion and place the items in order of importance from 1 to 10.

	Necessary	Desirable	Order of importance	
			Person A	Person B
Television				
Computer				
Home telephone				
Mobile phone				
Bed				
Hot water				
Drinking water				
Family car				
Heating				
Fridge				

9. How much did you agree with your partner?

10. One definition of poverty is 'the lack of basic necessities'.

    •   Is this a good definition?

    •   In your opinion, what are the 'basic necessities'?

    •   Do you think people experience poverty in your own community?

    •   Is there anything you can do to alleviate poverty?

Activity Sheet B
Shaheen's Story

Theme: Friendship

1. Imagine you are Shaheen and Tanya. Try out the scenario where Tanya tries to persuade Shaheen to go to the chicken shop to meet some boys (Scene J/Shaheen 4). Try out one of the the following different versions to help them to remain friendly:

   • Shaheen persuades Tanya not to go, but to have lunch in school to save money.

   • Shaheen refuses to go and Tanya goes on her own.

   • Tanya lends Shaheen money – to be paid back next week – so she can afford the chicken shop.

2. Hot-seat each other as the characters (i.e. one of you is the interviewer). How are the girls feeling about their friendship at the end of your version of the scenario?

3. Can you think of any other ways to play the scenario?

4. Find the best and most realistic scenario so that the girls remain friends?

5. Write a summary of Tanya and Shaheen's best way to sort out their differences in the box below.

6. Looking at the box above, can you imagine how other parts of Shaheen's life will be affected?

   • Her relationship with her Dad?

   • Her money problems?

   • Her success at school?

7. If you were Shaheen, how far would you go to keep a friend like Tanya? In what ways does money matter between friends?

8. Make a list of the qualities you have that make you a good friend. At the same time make a list of the qualities that make your partner a good friend. Compare your lists.

    •   Does your partner see you in the same light as you see yourself?

    •   How different are you as friends?

9. Can either of you think of examples from your own experiences of any of the following getting in the way of friendships?

	Yes/No
Families from different races and cultures	
Different religious backgrounds	
Having different amounts of money to spend	
Living in different areas	
Male/Female	
Dressing differently	
Liking different music	

10. Think about your school or youth centre. Are there practical things that could be done to make it friendlier?

Activity Sheet C
Mikey's Story

Theme: Housing

1. Imagine you're Mikey's Mum talking to a housing officer at the local council. Try different ways to play this scenario as Mum and the housing officer.

    *   Mum is very emotional

    *   Mum is calm

    *   The housing officer is sympathetic

    *   The housing officer is unsympathetic

2. Try out a scene where Mum tells Mikey what's happened after one of the scenes above.

    *   Is there a way that both Mikey and his Mum can 'win'?

    *   If not, what are the best compromises?

3. Here are some other solutions to Mikey's family's housing problems. Which do you think are the best and which the worst? There's also room for you to write your own suggestions.

Solution	How do you rate it?	
	Person A	Person B
Mikey moves out as soon as he's sixteen		
They rent a bigger house privately and Mikey gets a job to afford the extra cost		
They turn the sitting room into an extra bedroom		
Mary complains to the housing office that they've been treated unfairly.		

Did you agree with your partner?

4. How do the best of these solutions affect Mikey's other problems:

    •   Succeeding with his studies?

    •   Getting on with Jimmy?

    •   Having a good relationship with Tanya?

5. If you were Mikey, how would you feel about where you might live in the future – in say one, five or ten years time? Is there a problem of affordable housing in your area?

6. As well as the problem of sleeping rough, can you brainstorm other reasons why people might desperately need to move?

7. After you're eighteen, who is responsible for making sure you have decent housing? Look at the following statements. Put your initials on the grid in the box that is nearest to your opinion.

	AGREE	DISAGREE	UNSURE
We all have a responsibility for ourselves to get a good job to pay the rent or the mortgage			
Your parents should keep you under their roof until you can set yourself up			
Councils should provide affordable and decent housing for everyone			
Councils should only provide housing for people who are in desperate need			
Charities should provide housing for people in need.			

Did you agree with your partner?

8. Do you know what is going on in your area to help people with their housing needs?

- How does your area compare to the rest of the country?

- How does this country compare to the rest of the world?

- Do you have any practical suggestions for improving housing?

Activity Sheet D
Mikey's Story

Theme: Education

1. Imagine that you're Mikey and Ms Askew (Scene D/Mikey 2). Try one of these ways to play the scenario where Mikey asks for an extension on his project:

    •   Mikey threatens to complain to the headteacher or the school governors about the lack of support for his studies.

    •   Mikey refuses to leave the art room until his work is finished.

    •   Ms Askew is more sympathetic.

    •   Ms Askew is less sympathetic.

2. Hot-seat each other (one as one of the characters and the other as the interviewer). Find out how each character feels at the end of the scene.

3. Try out other scenarios to find the best solution to the problem.

4. What are the pressures on Ms Askew that make her seem unsympathetic to Mikey? Are these pressures the same in other schools?

5. Mikey is criticised by his Mum and his girlfriend for not concentrating enough on the 'core subjects' of Maths, English and Science.

    •   How realistic is his dream about becoming an artist?

    •   In your experience, does the curriculum have the right balance between subjects?

6. Make a secret list of the five best and five worst things about your school. Share it with your partner. How many things were the same?

7. How do you feel generally about the following statements about school? Put your initials in the box that is closest to your opinion.

	Agree	Disagree	Unsure
The best schools are the ones with the best results			
The best schools are the ones with the happiest pupils			
A school's main job is to prepare you for the world of work			
Schools should encourage you to challenge authority			
Schools should teach you to be obedient			
Schools should teach you to be a good citizen			
If you have ability, you will achieve at any school			
It is very hard to succeed in a bad school.			

Did you agree with your partner?

9. Think about your own school. Have you any practical suggestions to improve school life?

Activity Sheet E
Femi's Story

Theme: Police

1. Imagine you're Femi and PC Powell. Use the scenario where Femi gets arrested (Scene K/Femi3). Try out the following different versions:

    •   Femi accuses PC Powell of racism and threatens to bring a complaint against him.

    •   Femi is as polite as possible.

    •   PC Powell is as polite as possible.

2. Does Femi still get arrested when the scenario is played out in these ways? Is there a way for Femi to stand up for his rights and not get arrested?

3. What evidence does Femi have that PC Powell is prejudiced against him?

    •   Why might he judge Femi without knowing him?

    •   Is it because he's Black or young or with Paul Smith or any other reason?

    •   How can this kind of prejudice be challenged?

4. Do you imagine that Femi faces prejudice from people other than the police?

   • If so, who?

   • How does this compare with your own life?

   • Are there people who judge you before they know you?

5. Discuss any occasions when you've had dealings with the police.

   • Was the experience positive or negative?

   • Generally speaking, do you have confidence in the police?

   • Is this different in different areas?

   • How do you think the police in other countries compare to those in your own?

6. How do you feel about obeying the law?

   • Are there unjust laws?

   • Should you obey those?

7. Look at the following list of crimes and rank them in order of seriousness.

	How serious?	
	Person A	Person B
Burglary		
Assault		
Possession of cannabis		
Credit card fraud		
Fiddling an insurance claim		
Drinking and driving		
Mugging		
Speeding		
Computer hacking		

Did you agree with your partner?

8. What factors did you take into account to judge the seriousness of the crimes in exercise 7?

9. Discuss crime in your own community. If you were in charge of the local police and were given a fixed amount of money, what would your priorities be?

Activity Sheet F
Femi's Story

Theme: Activities for young people

1. Imagine a new scene. You are Paul and Femi and you are planning an evening's fun. Try this scenario in different ways: -

    •   You are both feeling negative about the possibilities.

    •   You are both feeling positive.

    •   One of you is positive, the other negative.

2. Discuss the different scenes you just tried out.

    •   What are the real options available to Paul and Femi?

    •   What factors limit their choice of activities?

3. Imagine you are Femi or Paul. What would be their idea of a brilliant evening? How similar or different is it from your own?

4. Write a short letter of complaint from an older neighbour to the police about Femi, Paul and other young people hanging out in the children's playground. Try to make it as realistic as possible.

5. Think about the activities you've done out of school in the past week and make a list of the first five that spring to mind.

    •   How many of them were based at home?

    •   How many do you think are paid for by your local council (e.g. a Youth Club or Swimming Pool)?

    •   How many are businesses run for profit (e.g. most cinemas, football clubs etc)?

Activity	Based at home	Funded by council	Private Business	Other/ Don't know
e.g. Ice-skating			✓	
1				
2				
3				
4				
5				

6. Discuss your findings with your partner.

    • Do you think there's enough to do in your area?

    • Is it affordable?

    • How many of the above activities would most adults approve of you doing?

    • How many do you think are educational?

7. Some people suggest that there's a link between activities for young people and crime? What do you think?

8. Are there particular streets, parks, shopping malls or other areas near you where young people hang out? Is this a problem or not?

9. What recommendation would you give to your local youth service to improve things for young people where you live?

6

Making Plays with Young People
– getting started

Devising plays: an overview

This chapter highlights some less obvious strategies for young people starting to create new plays linked to citizenship themes and issues.

The process of devising a play changes every time and, although techniques and approaches will be recycled and refined over several projects, each process will be unique to the group in question. Adapting approaches to suit context is therefore crucial. The processes can be undertaken with very diverse groups – from highly motivated and politicised to disenchanted young people and to a range of professional and aspiring professional performers. Working in the context of inner-city multicultural communities is my own experience, but I hope the content will stimulate group-leaders working in quite different circumstances.

In every instance, the creative process of making a play has the potential to promote learning on a number of interconnected and complementary levels:

- **aesthetically**: While shaping content for an audience, players must consider how to convey meaning. Is the intention to shock, amuse, unsettle, celebrate or move to tears? How can language, image, sound and movement combine to realise your intentions?

- **politically**: Each improvisation, discussion, scripting, design or music session will, on some level, demand that players develop their understanding of the social relationships and forces that affect the characters in their play. The workings of the state always impact on human stories, so a group-leader can draw this out of the process. Each fictional character and real-life player will have a relationship to laws, institutions and policy. It's at the point that character X goes to the doctor or character Y loses her job that social forces can be examined by the players-as-meaning-makers as part of a lively, playful and creative process.

- **communicatively**: The process of making a play is collaborative. The group-leader's main job is to encourage the group to tell the story well. For this to be achieved, each player needs to hone their interpersonal communication skills. Conflicts need to be managed, meaning negotiated and individual contributions encouraged. Establishing a culture of respect and generosity is paramount. This is clearly a transferable skill to many other contexts – particularly if we are to aspire to a society of active citizens participating in their communities.

Finding a balance between script and improvisation

This chapter is chiefly concerned with group work, so the role of the individual playwright is not referred to. Having the resource of an accomplished writer can certainly be productive (see Chapter 7) but there is always a danger that if the notion of collective authorship is not addressed at the start there will be little group ownership of the play.

It's wise never to be too dogmatic about the creation of scripts as part of the process of producing an original play. I've accomplished some successful processes that produced a show without any script. A group-leader might consider it pointless to script, particularly if the performers are improvising fluidly, maintaining effective performance rhythm and, especially, if a script is likely to create blocks and inhibitions. Although not standard practice in conventional theatre, much popular performance – stand-up comedy and storytelling for instance – maintains its freshness by using only brief structural notes as a skeleton guide. In fact *One Thursday* was only scripted after the first production was already in performance. The team realised that the show had found its own rhythm and structure through improvisation, and that the act of writing the script down and learning lines in a precise way was unnecessary and potentially unhelpful. There might also be performances where technical and stage management workers are the only people to have a scripted record of the words and actions in the show – purely as a sensible method for effecting scene changes and lighting/sound cues.

When considering whether to write or to devise, it's worth reflecting on the positive attributes of both processes and seeing how they can be usefully combined.

Writing
- Encourages young people's literacy skills

- Essential for precision in the case of highly rhythmic and some stylised language – such as raps, poems and song lyrics

- Written dialogue is often pacier and crisper than some improvisations, which can tend to ramble and bore an audience

- Creatively suits the young people who prefer the private act of writing to the public act of discussion, debate and negotiation

- Recording the speech and actions on stage can cement a process that is otherwise easily forgotten, particularly if the group is meeting sporadically and not rehearsing over a solid block of time.

Devising
- Can be a process where the group feels a great sense of collective ownership of the show

- Can usefully emphasise non-verbal communication – creating meaning with images and movement as well as words

- Can tap into the intuitive skills of a group and their own cultural forms – such as freestyle rapping, comedy improvisation, storytelling and street dance

- Can unlock the expressive abilities of young people who are afraid of the written word

- A purely devised show can be created surprisingly quickly. And it avoids that sticky, de-motivating time in rehearsal when people haven't learned their lines and also the embarrassment of 'drying' in performance.

Whichever emphasis you place on the process, it is worth realising that a writer usually needs some form of collaboration with other artists to produce a good play. By contrast, most devised plays need someone in the team who can have a sense of overview, noting the most effective fragments and editing them into a coherent whole.

Using consistent and effective theatrical conventions
My own preference with work with young people is for portable and simple theatrical effects. In my experience, too many groups shift their focus from the essential elements of drama – story, character, theme and image – to dwell on received ideas about theatrical presentation, especially elaborate and distracting props and costumes.

I've mostly found it useful to introduce simple and consistent theatrical conventions that can hold a story together and trigger the imagination of the players. I can recall a memorable art class as a child where the teacher told us all that we were only to use black and white paints. After much groaning and complaining at the lack of freedom this imposed on us, we all knuckled down to the task. Gradually, we became aware that just these two colours in our palette yielded infinite variations in terms of shades of grey. Eventually the monochrome works were displayed – to great admiration. The constraints had actually enabled us all to unlock an element of our imagination we had failed to activate before. This guiding principle of the creative process – that 'limitation is stimulation' – applies as much to the making and teaching of theatre as any other art form.

Limitation also encourages a consistent use of conventions. A sudden shift in conventions – say the introduction of song in an otherwise naturalistic piece – can unnerve an audience and detract from the main mission to tell a story interestingly.

It's also worth noting that style can be effectively integrated from the beginning of a devising process, remembering that theatre is a multi-arts discipline. Words are only one element used to make meaning and players can also experiment with the visual/spatial and musical/sound dimensions of performance as an integrated part of the devising process.

Bearing this in mind, design and music considerations can be introduced early on in the devising process:

•   Is there a DJ amongst the young people you work with? Can they spontaneously find rhythms, mood music and sound effects that hold the scenes together?

•   Is there one song, rhythmic idea or sound pattern that can punctuate scenes?

•   Is there a simple design concept that you can use? What effects can be achieved using just bamboo canes or cardboard boxes or bubble wrap or sheets? Can you limit yourself to two colours? Is there a way of using simple projection restricted to only black and white photographs? Is there a theatre designer or visual artist who could help you? Which of these conventions will add something to your show?

•   How will the young people get on and off the performing area? Is there a simple convention that could add something to the style and symbolism of the piece without the distraction of players moving on and off and the time that takes? Maybe they could all come from the audience or be placed at the side or back of the space all the time?

•   Do you have to create your show 'end on' – or can the audience be on two, three or four sides?

Whatever conventions you set out, the focus should be on serving the on-stage action and narrative.

Finding content through expressive exercises

Although many citizenship and drama projects will start by deliberating on specific issues, a devising process can allow content to emerge from a group by exploring expressive considerations. You may find, for example, that an introductory session is best run from the point of view of design or music. This may produce ideas that would never be conceived when your group is working on explicit issues or as performers in a standard improvisation and, indeed, may stimulate a different perspective on the issues when they naturally appear.

The examples in Chapter Seven will show processes where citizenship, in a number of different ways, is an explicit and core purpose to the project. By contrast, this chapter shows how, in a way, all theatre-making deals with our role in society and that this can emerge more subtly by focusing primarily on the role of the artist.

Setting up a process that is openly creative can be especially useful to counteract 'issue fatigue'. I have a vivid memory of a young woman in a special school, when I'd first been introduced as a drama worker.

'You come 'ere to do stuff about AIDS? We done that already!'

The assumption knocked me back.

'No, we've come to do a play. It can be about whatever you want.'

It was clear that she was suspicious of drama – a process that might be used to preach covertly about issues important to the teacher.

If a teacher or group-leader has a relatively open brief, then he or she can trust that the content latent in any group will start to present itself in the stories they choose. It's then up to the group-leader to draw out the citizenship issues.

Devising strategies to generate content

The following examples demonstrate ways to start with expressive exercises – focusing on a simple creative process – so a group's own issues come to the surface organically. The exercises use a multi-arts approach, so can be tailored to suit the group and the group-leader's skills and disposition. Players are en- couraged to think in pictures, rhythms and sound as well as words. Doing so can lead to a more creative process than pure discussion formats:

- **Theme tunes** – each player thinks of a song to be the theme tune for a character. Whilst travelling across the space together, the players play the song to themselves in their heads, humming it to themselves if necessary. Gradually they let the song inform their movement as they undertake a variety of everyday physical tasks: say, getting ready in the morning or doing a day's work. The idea of letting rhythm and melody inform a physical attitude will be second nature to anyone who has used a personal stereo. Then each player devises a short solo movement piece to depict their character and other players reflect on what they see. At this point the narrative can start to come into the foreground of the work.

'Where is the character going?'

'Where has she come from?'

And with narrative, themes start to flow:

'Why is she worried?'

'What has made him feel so superior?'

And so a narrative emerges that is based on character. Gradually characters can meet each other, still using the abstract stimulus of their theme tunes. This exercise might well inform the use of music in your final piece.

- **Soundscape** – see if the group can tell a story using just sound with no words or actions. This exercise can be used as a starting point or later on in the process to give shape, pace and rhythm to a section.

- **Table-top show** – try creating a scene as a tabletop performance. In small groups, miniature characters are created, made out of simple materials such as plasticine. You can give each group a guiding limitation. Maybe all the characters are a family, a group of friends or work colleagues. The setting can be made out of any available scaled-down materials – matchboxes, cutlery, yoghurt pots. The players play out a scene in the way small children play with dolls and objects – animating the characters and speaking for them. This can be explored as a spontaneous improvisation and shared amongst the group.

- **Wordless table-top** – try combining the last two exercises by letting your tabletop performance be improvised without words. It's worth observing how infants play spontaneously with objects to create the feel of this exercise.

- **Opening stage direction** – place two everyday objects, say a wastepaper bin and a chair, in an area designated as the stage. Invite a member of the group to arrange these two objects in relation to each other in any way that's interesting. Each player must now imagine that this is the opening image of a play. Each player writes the first stage direction for the play, involving one or two characters. They must stop writing after the first character speaks. These fragments are presented and the gathering then speculates about how the play might continue. As well as being a powerful stimulus for narrative, this exercise demonstrates the potential for the symbolic resonance of objects placed in a performing space and how much meaning can be conveyed through actions rather than words.

- **Outline characters** – in pairs, players draw round each other's bodies to create a life-size outline. Each then fills in their own shape using colours and textures. The objective is to express how you see yourself and deal with the world in a semi-abstract way. The careful choice of colours and materials is therefore essential to open up creative possibilities. The outlines are cut out and exhibited around the space. The group comments on the feelings expressed and the characters that are developing. These are now differentiated, living characters. The discussion can now divert from a discussion of individual players to these new differentiated characters. Now the group can place the characters in relation to each other and to objects in the room. Are fragments of narrative appearing? Can interesting conflicts and dilemmas be projected onto the characters? How might we develop the images into fuller dramas? Can this exercise inform the costume convention of a play?

- **Shrines** – players are invited to collect usable objects that might signify a character. These can be three-dimensional found objects – a leaf, a box of matches and a tube of toothpaste, for example. Two-dimensional images and fragments of language cut from magazines and newspapers can also be used, but players should be encouraged to use words minimally. A 'shrine' is then constructed to represent the character. The objects are placed in conjunction with each other and modified or adapted to create a sense of that person. The objective is not to create a realistic model of the person but rather an impression of their emotional and social being. Players can be invited to find a suitable location for their shrine – a particularly effective exercise if you have access to interesting sites and locations outside a standard classroom or rehearsal space. The group is then taken on a guided tour of the shrines. Although each player will be anxious to describe their own work, it can be more revealing if each has the task of interpreting someone else's creation. The act of interpretation can itself move the work from the private to the public sphere and lead on to making connections between the characters. Polaroid photographs can be taken of each shrine and a collective image created. Players are encouraged to extend the characters' lives into narrative as the start of devising scenes. It may even be worth reviewing the shrines at a later date when considering stage design.

- **Clapping conversation** – in pairs, players create an abstract clapping conversation. One player claps any rhythm or sequence and their partner answers. This should occur spontaneously, without premeditation. Each player must tune in to their partner until they really feel that they're playing the same scene. No words can be used. The players carry on this abstract conversation until they feel that the exchange has reached a natural conclusion. They reflect on the relationship. If a group is confident about working together, some of these clapping conversations can be tried out in front of the rest of the group for them to interpret what they observe. These relationships can then be re-interpreted as improvised scenes.

• **More wordless conversations** – the idea of an abstract wordless conversation can be explored in other ways. Players can for example use musical instruments. Or pairs of players balance a bamboo pole between them, using only their index fingers, and try moving around the space without dropping the pole. An instant power relationship begins – a dialogue of negotiated leadership. By starting with an abstract game, players can find a natural, instinctive playfulness where human relationships are primarily expressed in terms of rhythm. These exercises resonate with lived experience. A player might achieve ascendancy in the bamboo game by lowering herself and forcing her partner to stretch uncomfortably high. On reflection, this dialogue might be found to contain the essential dynamics that, say, are present when a teacher gives a pupil an impossible task to complete. When constructing this explicit scene through improvisation, the bamboo game will elicit previously unimaginable nuances.

• **Very quick stories** – this exercise owes a lot to Vivian Gussin Paley's (1990) techniques of storytelling/storyacting with early years. In pairs, players tell each other stories. The stories can be about anything, as long as they've really happened. The listener/player must employ active listening techniques – questioning to clarify and enable the teller/player. The listener/players know that they will need to retell the stories in just *thirty* seconds in the next phase of the exercise. So, as practice for the next bit, the stories are retold in the pairs as thirty-second 'pitches' in the manner of a Hollywood screenwriter. The group-leader marks out a square on the floor to indicate the stage space and the players sit evenly spaced around the square with their thirty-second pitches prepared. Each player in turn relays the pitch they've just heard within the time limitation. After hearing it, the group tries to enact the story spontaneously – the players being encouraged to jump into the square and become the characters. The object is – as a group – to act out the stories as a fast as possible. The group-leader encourages all the players to participate fully. With a group of more than twelve players, it becomes difficult for everyone to have the time to share a story. Group-leaders may feel torn between deepening experiences and democratising them. 'Quick stories' is good way to value contributions fairly. Then the group can draw out narrative and thematic threads in the various stories .... and the devising process has begun.

This list of devising games and exercises is by no means exhaustive. Group-leaders can refer to a number of other books for further inspiration, some of which are contained in the bibliography. In addition, it may be useful to use these techniques as a basis for your own refinements, based on experience. Inevitably, the rituals, tempo and tone of these techniques will suit different group-leaders in different ways and it is important that group-leaders can develop the confidence to adapt liberally.

7

Making Plays with Young People – creating performance

Thisis chapter describes a selection of my own theatre projects. Though most were carried out before the new Citizenship curriculum was proposed, these examples nonetheless shed light on the educational and artistic processes of devising theatre on citizenship themes. I hope that by seeing specific drama strategies and planning ideas put in context, readers will be helped to transfer some of these approaches, general and specific, to their own work.

I have organised the chapter according to the projects' starting points or initial impulses. Sometimes the starting point for a project appears as a given – the context dictates it. For example, specified funding or an organisational mission often define the starting point, for, say, a health, literacy, crime or careers initiative. These external constraints may seem far removed from a group's day to day experience, but can generally be creatively embraced and adapted for the greater good of the players' learning. By contrast, other projects will begin with no such constraints, leaving the group and its leader to locate their own starting point and direction. Whatever the history and context of a project, I hope that the following stories show that the most successful work has group investment and involvement at its heart.

Starting points for writing and devising processes

Existing expressed issues: a weekend residency for London Borough of Waltham Forest

The Youth Service for the London Borough of Waltham Forest invited my Theatre Royal Stratford East team to work over a weekend with a specially recruited group of young people. Our task was to start the process of building a drama-based voluntary youth forum on local issues. The twelve young volunteers reflected the geographical, cultural and educational diversity of the borough and were drama and citizenship enthusiasts.

During the residency, I used a team of skilled young professionals – a singer, a drama worker, a DJ and a dancer – selected for their energy and understanding of youth culture. Local youth workers who joined us made an important pastoral contribution and ensured the continuity of the project.

On arrival at our splendidly equipped residential setting, we set out our mission for the weekend – to have fun and work hard to achieve something to be proud of.

Following a playful session on group dynamics and ground rules, we introduced the topics for the weekend. Our initial stimulus was a bar chart showing the results of earlier research. The four areas of most concern to local youth were education, policing, youth activities and safety on the streets. Through our recruitment workshops, we knew these four areas to be of major importance to our group too. So these four generalised themes provided a focused framework to generate specific theatrical statements using narrative, music and image.

We started by labelling each corner of the room with one of these issues and invited the group to respond instantly and honestly to a range of statements:

'Go to the corner you know most about personally.'

'Go to the corner which makes you most angry.'

'Go to the corner you care most about.'

'Go to the corner you care least about.'

'Make a still image in any corner, showing a powerless person.'

'Make a still image in any corner, showing a powerful person.'

'Make a still image of yourself in any corner.'

This exercise was punctuated with rhythmic walking around the room accompanied by carefully chosen music from our DJ – a Theatre Royal Stratford East youth theatre graduate DJ Excalibah. When each physical 'statement' had been made, each player was invited to observe the whole group response.

It's interesting to note how this lively, physically based activity stimulates learning in three distinct but complementary ways:

- The first act, of walking and considering the statements, stimulates each person to engage in internal, contemplative learning. So it's important not to rush the activity. The group-leader's coaching abilities and the accompanying music are thus critical to creating an unselfconscious atmosphere.

- The second phase of making a physical choice – initially by placing yourself in a corner and later by creating an expressive image – commits the players to making a public statement. This is within the comfort of what Christine Poulter (1987) calls a 'low focus' activity, where everyone is doing the same thing simultaneously minimising exposure for an individual.

- In the final, reflective phase a moment is given for the group to see how others have responded. The individual statement is now part of a group kaleidoscope. The temptation is resisted to open discussion at this point; instead the images speak for themselves. The rhythm of the exercise could easily be disrupted and its egalitarian nature jeopardised by the more talkative members in the group, but the music keeps them on task.

Following the four corners exercise, our group expanded their understanding of these issues by creating short pieces in small groups of three striking still images, rhythmically linked with movement and music from DJ Excalibah. Each of these short pieces reflected the groups' lived experience of the themes.

The structure for the weekend was loosely based on exploring real stories of 'today' and imagined improvements for 'tomorrow'. The short pieces surprised and impressed us with their power and subtlety. When we all went to bed at last, exhausted, we knew there was a strong basis for a powerful theatrical statement. A statement based not on the naturalism to which many young people are instinctively drawn but on a more expressionistic style that employed a 'hip-hop' sensibility encouraged by the collaboration with DJ Excalibah.

Our first session on the Saturday morning took a more traditional lesson-style format -exploring the difference and relationship between campaigning and lobbying:

- Campaigning was defined as: getting others to support you

- Lobbying as: influencing decision-makers so they will back your cause.

This topic was related back to our emerging piece of theatre and its potential to activate and influence others. This session was congruent with our aim of not only producing a piece of engaging theatre but also providing the means for the group to use it locally for active citizenship.

Saturday afternoon entailed some polishing of the stylised mini-scenes devised the previous night. Singer Marilyn Gentle had composed a simple refrain that could link the scenes and provide a powerful leitmotif for the piece. The act of ensemble singing was a useful up-beat collective activity and the single line – 'I see you listening, but do you hear me!' – synthesised the group's strong feelings about the condescending attitude to young people characteristic of adults in power.

With confidence and group cohesion high, we started on the more difficult task of formulating solutions/improvements to the real problems presented in the mini-scenes. It was much easier for the group to agree about what 'today's' problems were. After all, it is difficult to disagree with an authentic narrative. But when asked 'what is to be done?' about the complexity of the practical relationships between the people in power, those they rule over/serve and the management of resources can leave everyone feeling frustrated and confused.

During our discussions, we encouraged the young people to chair and manage their own discussions – to try to replicate the democratic sensibility we had promoted in the drama-based and non-verbal exercises. Our discussions on solutions/improvements were predictably inconclusive, but they enabled us to see that the creation of specific policy and legislation was beyond our power during the weekend.

To give them an entertaining and enjoyable exercise that would make progress on the solutions/improvements, I asked each group to explore a positive future using a 'sketch' format. We discussed how our favourite sketches from TV shows such as 'Goodness Gracious Me' work – looking particularly at irony and metaphor. This idea took hold with the group, tapping into the comedic sense so often employed to good effect during their recreational time.

The 'education' group had been discussing the extent to which they were 'customers' in their schools. I suggested that this might translate into an interesting sketch format. They duly produced a pair of contrasting scenes using the metaphorical setting of a fast-food restaurant. The first scene showed a disgruntled pupil/customer asking for items that were not on offer. The following extract always raised a laugh in performance:

SHOPPER: Do you do languages?

STAFF: Yeah.

SHOPPER: Oh good. I'd like some Chinese please – the most spoken language in the world. A large portion of that. A spattering of Spanish. Bit of Yoruba and some sign language.

STAFF: We don't do them.

SHOPPER: What do you do then?

STAFF: French.

[She mimes putting down a large heavy package.]

SHOPPER: And....

STAFF: Just French.

The contrasting Utopian 'tomorrow' sketch contained the following:

SHOPPER: I'd like some history please.

STAFF: Certainly. What kind can I get you madam?

SHOPPER: (Tentatively) Do you have any Black history?

STAFF: Oh yes. Black British. Black African. Black Caribbean. Black American.
           We've got them all.

SHOPPER: I'd like a bit of each of those. And a bit of English Kings and Queens
           thrown in.

STAFF: (Miming providing a mixed package of goodies) There you go.

SHOPPER: How much is that?

STAFF: It's free of course. A pleasure to serve you!

On the Sunday we connected the stylised mini-scenes with the comedy sketches, and rehearsed and polished the whole show. The Theatre Royal's Marketing and Press Officer Kim Morgan made a guest appearance to talk about attracting an audience and how to work with politicians. This inspired the group to start the process of discussing the political and cultural value of touring the new piece to other young people and inviting local politicians as part of a lobbying process on key issues.

At the time of writing, the experiment of combining drama and citizenship work is continuing with Waltham Forest Youth Service. Although the piece we put together over the weekend didn't sustain a substantial tour, a second, similar drama project exploring Safety on the Streets has since been completed by the Theatre Royal team, and a larger and more active group combining the two projects is now in progress.

Although the process was clearly valuable for the young people taking part, it remains to be seen whether the more ambitious aim can be achieved: namely, to produce a sustainable theatre group of young people who can facilitate real political change in their community.

The unexpressed issues: Akton Kultural Assembley

As youth workers and teachers, we're often frustrated by the apparent lack of self-awareness of a particular group of young people. Often we see damaging patterns of behaviour being repeated. A particular prejudice or set of prejudices, for example, can become ingrained in the group culture through the exchange of insults and the marginalisation of more vulnerable group members. In the context of my most recent work in East London, what particularly comes to mind are homophobic insults, attention-seeking behaviour by young men in mixed groups that inhibits the contributions of the young women – and many shades of direct and indirect racism.

One of the most revealing instances of racial intolerance I've encountered was whilst putting together a large-scale community show with young people on the South Acton Estate in West London for the London Bubble Theatre Company. My chief collaborator on the project was performer/workshop leader Tony Gouveia, and we had the support of a team made up of a designer, community workers, actors and technicians. We worked through local schools and youth organisations to create a team of performers, with the intention of celebrating the diversity in their area. The time and resource parameters of the project meant we had to work with our different groups separately, bringing them together at the end of the process for only one evening of performance and entertainment.

After an initial round of taster workshops with various identified groups, our team met to decide on a holding form for the show. We were particularly despondent at the appalling internal dynamics of the groups. Tony had noticed that there was particular resentment and antagonism between different groups of black young people. A number of the young people of mixed parentage were insulted as not being 'black enough' to meet the approval of some of the others. In turn, these young people had retaliated by using the word 'African' as a term of abuse, in the effort to protect their dignity. This dynamic was in the foreground of our experiences and had succeeded in overshadowing the needs of the other young people from varied backgrounds: white, middle-eastern, Asian and Filipino, among others. How, in this context, could we create an event that celebrated the cultures of the estate and surrounding area, without inadvertently inflaming already volatile emotions?

We were concerned that a direct expression of individual cultures – say through learning songs and dances from around the world – might expose individuals in the group to ridicule. Instead, we decided to explore the issue obliquely, creating a framework to look at culture and nationality in their widest senses.

Each separate group was therefore set the task of creating a fictional country which would be invited to present an expression of their culture through song, dance and drama. We presented the groups with different starting points. One group looked at how climate might effect culture and they decided that their country was plagued with excessive rainfall. Their final presentation was an eccentric and energetic dance involving umbrellas, wellies and raincoats. Another group looked at how their society came to make decisions and invented a system of ultra-democratic government where every member of the community was forced to wear an oversized collar whenever they spoke. This group used a comedy-sketch format to present their idea.

The whole performance was achieved in the round, using the conventions of the United Nations as a theatrical holding form; each country had designed its own flag and the 'delegates' sat at an official desk and observed each others' performance. The event was topped off by the surprise appearance of a manic robot (constructed by the young people who preferred not to perform) which threatened an immediate coup. Through the power of song – all the players in full voice – the robot was defeated and dramatically expired.

The only element of the event that showed the diversity of authentic cultures on the estate was the feast prepared by the parents of the players. This went a long way to representing the real diversity of the gathering: the array of dishes and the disco that followed celebrated all the contributors' achievements.

Using this event as a starting point, local networks set up a more permanent youth arts group and our team moved on to another project elsewhere.

One unsatisfactory element of this way of working is the absence of any assessment of the long-term impact of these one-off projects – particularly in terms of success in such learning areas as challenging prejudice. Our aim was to create an exciting learning experience which would operate on a subconscious level. We made a clear decision not to confront the prejudices we encountered overtly, thinking that doing so would, at best, result in a show depicting the 'teacher's answer' – with players spending the process presenting us with the views and ideas they thought we wanted to hear. In a sense, we created a parallel world to explore alternative human relationships to the reality as perceived by this community. This way of working is in line with one of the essential propositions of drama work: that a fictional distance liberates people to explore their current predicaments. However, as we worked in a theatrical rather than dramatic process, the learning areas were never explicitly flushed out and examined in the light of lived experience. We hoped that the experience of celebrating together with the people they had previously felt antagonistic towards would be powerful enough to contribute to challenging prejudice.

This example also demonstrates that an advantage of both drama and theatre is that topics can be approached obliquely. Subconsciously, the fictional activity will encourage comparison with, and thus increased understanding of, the actual experience of each participant and audience member. As each person's experience is different, the effect of the dramatic activity on his or her development will be unique. This is not the world of 'right answers' that is comfortable for those seeking measurable outcomes. However, anecdotal evidence would suggest that drama projects of this kind are often cited as amongst the most memorable formative educational experiences.

The given issue: Jack the Biscuit

At the end of the twentieth century, with 'loose' funding for expressive arts projects being squeezed by successive administrations, those interested in educational drama found themselves working within the 'tight' funding of schemes such as drugs prevention initiatives. *Jack the Biscuit* was one such project.

It is still the case that group-leaders may have a proscribed starting point as the result of a governmental or institutional initiative. These initiatives are frequently driven by health concerns. The social and emotional impact of issues such as drugs and sexual health are effectively explored through drama, as well as offering hard information about benefit and harm.

These issues are undoubtedly of interest and concern to young people – after all resources have usually been made available because a legitimate need has been recognised. The premise that drama engages young people in a unique and effective way can lead to a simplistic assumption that drama can in some way convert young people to a legitimised view on a specific topic. But this is not necessarily so. What drama does is to bring complexities to the surface – certainty is seldom an appropriate starting point. After all, we are dealing with the imprecise business of emotions, aesthetics and human behaviour.

In terms of a model for citizenship education, we should perhaps cautiously welcome these initiatives, while at the same time insisting that drama be used to interrogate the certainties of the state by setting them against the uncertainties of lived experience.

Jack the Biscuit was a show devised by young people as part of the Home Office Drugs Prevention Initiative. It exemplified how such projects can be both liberating and constraining.

I was offered a small grant to work with young people at Hoxton Hall – a community arts centre in East London. The agency worker presented the grant as peculiarly unrestricted.

'You're working with young people at risk of getting involved with drugs. Our money will help you to provide activity for them. Keeps them occupied. Keeps them away from drugs. The content is up to you. I know it's just a small grant, but if we like what we see, there's a chance of building on this work.'

My team thought about this proposition and our own desire to attract young people to come and use the building. We wanted to focus our attention on those who were hanging out at the neighbouring arcade and becoming involved with a range of activities that put them at risk of being arrested and embroiled with the criminal justice system. The daily routine for this group of young people was to skip school in the afternoon, earn some money by stealing a car stereo, smoke cigarettes and joints, spend their money on gambling machines and cans of cheap beer and, maybe, get into a fight with young people from neighbouring estates in the evening. Yes, a few of the young people were taking harder drugs – but the central problem here was not the one identified by the state.

We discussed the matter further and decided we would use the grant to create a show exploring 'instant gratification culture' – the factor we felt to be under-lying the range of problems faced by this group. Their day to day lives revolved around the need for immediate excitement. Because the message given to them by professional adults didn't match their experiences, this was understandable. Teachers, youth workers, social workers and others kept extolling the virtues of education, qualifications and diligence. But their experience had taught them that the price they paid in boredom and peer derision was in no way com-pensated by promises of a 'good job'.

It was also difficult to engage this group with arts work. Many of them would say that they aspired to become musicians, for example, but the discipline of learning technique was too demanding to be contemplated. Creating a show might well generate a level of excitement to compete with daily activities, but the work needed would probably present too great a challenge. And if the result-ing performance was unimpressive, then trust in us could be lost – after all, what's the point of working hard to create something if the result is inadequate? We therefore needed to find a way of working that would incrementally increase the level of commitment – and gamble that the end product would instil a sense of collective pride.

We constructed a process founded on two fundamental principles:

• The project would be run by a steering group of young people already enthusiastic about the arts. These should be peers who were respected by the group who were not active in the centre.

• Content should be unrestricted and uncensored – chosen by the group and facilitated by the workshop-leaders.

I presented the project as comparable to a live documentary – a chance to pre-sent the world from the perspective of the young people of Hoxton. We gathered a panorama of stories from the young people; unsurprisingly these stories revolved around the instant gratification culture. We gathered ideas for scenes in a number of imaginative ways – for example, setting up a video in the style of

Crimewatch and eliciting evidence in the manner of a witness in silhouette. Our core group worked on translating the evidence into high quality dramatic vignettes, pinning the real experiences onto three archetypal characters. Gradually, the core group expanded as those hanging out outside the centre became interested in the developing show. Finally, several months later, we were ready for an audience.

The final piece was entitled *Jack the Biscuit* – named after a pejorative phrase used by the group to describe someone who thinks too well of themselves. There were scenes about the unique street language involved in sharing a packet of cigarettes, about how a car is chosen for its stereo to steal and about the lure of heroin. The group had also created slides of local landmarks and rehearsed songs to accompany the piece. The audience of young people and their friends, relatives and neighbours from the local community appreciated the show hugely. The young people were elated. A good many of them had learned to trust the process – and they had been rewarded with a new buzz.

I approached one of the Home Office drugs workers after the show, in the hope of acquiring more funding to take these young people out of London and show our work to a wider audience.

'Very nice. But it wasn't really about primary drugs prevention.'

'I'm sorry.... I didn't realise.'

'Yes, well. We've been given a directive. We should channel funds into schemes that can show hard outcomes in terms of stopping young people taking drugs. The stuff in your show about cigarettes, drink and friendship isn't what we're after. Have you thought about getting the kids to design a poster that says 'just say no'?'

This experience highlights some general principles. We are often asked to tackle a single issue through drama and theatre and this can initially seem appealing. But when devising shows with young people, it is vital that they be engaged with the topic on their own terms. We must explore beyond the surface needs of the state to deal with anti-social and damaging behaviour quickly and not promise that drama will deliver instant outcomes. Indeed, such changes may not even be measurable in the short term. We must be prepared to embrace contradictions and explore their implications and to be clear that there is no definitive answer to questions about human behaviour.

So, if you're faced with the prospect of responding to a broad agenda, it may be useful to reframe the concern in a meaningful way for your group. Just as *Jack the Biscuit* came out of re-positioning a drugs initiative so as to explore more broadly the identified instant gratification culture, so the starting point for, say, a sexual health project with young women might be 'pressure on girls', 'when do I become a woman?' or 'am I becoming my mother?' The choice that is likely to be successful will be the one that reflects the young people's world perspectives rather than the exigencies of government.

Latching on to educational initiatives can give rise to one of the most unconsidered approaches to devising plays with young people. That is to start by trying to articulate the 'message'. What if the group doesn't all agree with the message? And what difference will it make to an audience who already agree or disagree? If we are given a starting point, perhaps the best way to proceed is to ascertain the underlying human questions that will resonate with the group and to begin with our own discovery as group-leaders.

The documentary approach: Means to an End

Means to an End was a show devised and written by professional actors working interactively with pensioners in Birmingham. Although this show was produced by adults for audiences aged over fifty, the processes are applicable to work with young people.

Most groups of young people will be familiar with the idea of documentary through television and this can be an accessible way to introduce the idea of documentary drama – particularly as television documentary has become more overtly entertaining in recent years.

It's worth emphasising that documents are highly effective as a starting point and that there are many ways to use them to create live performance. The notion of journalistic integrity and respecting authenticity can be useful and can be used with some degree of dramatic licence to create an entertaining result.

The act of research is also an invaluable part of the learning process. Documents can be interestingly generated from a variety of sources, and research doesn't have to be limited to the historical archive of a library. Useful documents can include sound recordings, videos, photographs, newspapers, websites and other stimuli. The group can also generate its own documents by interviewing living witnesses, using a range of media.

Many a devising process has got bogged down in the need to read large and worthy tomes on a given issue and so we should focus on the kinds of document that are more likely to produce effective results. Intellectual analyses and records of data and statistics may have limited theatrical uses, unless clearly connected to the stories of real people. Verbatim first person narratives, accounts of incidents, video documentaries and photographs may be much more likely to inspire a group to create engaging theatre.

Once an array of enticing documents has been assembled, the players should be encouraged to use these creatively. For example:

• A certain player can effectively perform a first person narrative as a monologue. The group can experiment with different ways this can be achieved. What if the actor is totally different from the character – a different gender or ethnic group, for example? What if the speech is accompanied by contrasting images, projected on a screen or embodied by performers? How might music enhance the effect of the narrative?

• Use a photograph as the stimulus for a dance or movement piece. Could you, for example, use Robert Capa's war photographs for this purpose?

• Look at the way newspapers and magazines cover a hot issue. For example, the sentencing of child 'offenders'. Who do these media quote and how are people differently portrayed? Try to create some theatrical statements using only sentences appearing in these newspapers, contrasting different perspectives and reporting styles. The players can use scissors, paste and photocopies to create a script, adding no words of their own, but with freedom to juxtapose their own images, sound and movement.

The aesthetic choices inherent in these ways of working inevitably deepen the citizenship learning, especially if harnessed to reveal the truth of the particular issue. The group can imagine themselves to be fictional Martians, coming to Earth to discover the essence of the issue unhindered by history and prejudice.

There have been a number of notable models of documentary drama that have emphasised the importance of 'actuality' – maintaining the integrity of the original speech and meaning of real people. This technique has produced some very exciting and influential theatre at the Victoria Theatre, Stoke on Trent and at Banner Theatre in Birmingham, for example.

My preference as a theatre-maker, however, has been to favour 'artistic' over 'journalistic' integrity – using documents to stimulate an imaginative process which will get an audience engaged and provoked by an issue. In a sense, Joan Littlewood and Theatre Workshop's classic show 'Oh What a Lovely War' is the first and possibly most enduring example of this attitude to document.

How then do you choose a topic that would benefit from a documentary approach? In many ways, by choosing this way of working you have already decided that your group would benefit from a distancing from their subject. It is likely that none of your group have a great deal of direct experience of the topic – or they would be the information source for the research – and that you are hoping they will benefit from empathy and a more objective perspective. As with much other theatre and citizenship work, the choice of topic may well be related to the group's abiding concerns and attitudes.

For example, you might want to challenge the negative view of refugees that prevails. There are many documents available that tell authentic and contemporary stories of refugees, available from bodies such as the Refugee Council. Although useful, you may judge them to be too close to home. So you might look at more distanced documents, such as experiences from other countries and times, that could make it easier for you to engage with universal themes of nationality, xenophobia and displacement.

One of the most effective ways to generate documents for a devising and writing process is through recording the testimony of people who have first hand experience. This can be achieved in many ways, such as using a dictaphone and sympathetically questioning the person concerned.

One of my earliest experiences of devising in this way was creating a show called *Means to an End* with Bread and Circuses Theatre Company in Birmingham. Our starting point was an interest in the growth of the welfare state and we wanted to use stories from local pensioners. Our first attempts to gather material were severely hampered by a group of elders who were more interested in bingo than reminiscence. I soon discovered that what interested me didn't necessarily interest the people it had happened to.

I'll never forget one of the most extraordinary exchanges I've ever taken part in – maybe this should have become dialogue in a show:

> 'I've not done that much in my life. Just fought in three wars and gone down the pit' – said without a trace of irony.
>
> 'Three wars!'
>
> 'Oh yes. First, Second and Spanish Civil. Now, if you don't mind, bingo's about to start.'

Despite the realisation that there are those who prefer not to tell their stories and that this needs to be respected and permission sought to use testimony, we persisted with this group.

Our first round of chats did produce some fragments of narrative and anecdotes. One of the most interesting concerned childbirth.

> 'Course children was never born in hospital. There was always a woman in the street who came round to deliver.'
>
> 'A midwife?'

'Gracious no! She'd just learnt it from her mother, I suppose.'

When this fragment was taken back to the rehearsal room, we realised we needed a lot more detail to fashion a convincingly authentic scene. We decided to create a short model scene to present to our group the following week. The scene would deliberately contain gaps and flagrantly inauthentic elements. We hoped this would cajole the group into helping us to devise a scene that would be recognisable to other people who had lived through similar circumstances.

So, careful not to disrupt the bingo again, we presented a short improvisation, set on the night when mother's waters broke. Jan Bessant played the part suitably graphically, Spud Murphy clowning around as her husband, hopeless in the face of nature's urgency and certainty. At a key point in the action, Spud turned to the audience – now howling with laughter – and asked for their advice:

'Shall I call a doctor?'

'You can't afford a doctor!' yelled back someone in the front row.

'And you ain't got a telephone!' added another.

'What should I do? Is there a midwife?'

'Didn't have such a thing,' came the retort.

'Go out in the street and knock up the woman next door. She'll deliver the baby.'

I stopped the scene and pointed out that we didn't have any actors who would know how to play the woman next door. Without any persuasion, Beryl briskly made her way onto the performing area and offered to show us how it was done. She joined in with the improvisation and helped Jan to give birth to a beautiful baby boy. The group loved the experience so much that bingo started late that day.

Back in the rehearsal room, we realised that Beryl had given us a physical document – one that would have been unobtainable from any other source. Jan, who had already given birth to a real son of her own, told us that the physical act of midwifery as demonstrated by Beryl was wholly different to contemporary practice. It was clearly expert, but it involved the woman next door pulling the mother's legs over her head and involving herself in a whole host of other rituals that were abandoned once the health service was established.

Our show – *Means to an End* – used this experience to create a scene that was uniquely recognisable to our audience as authentic. It also helped us as a team to understand the complexity of the issue. Yes, the health service has been a huge boon to the health of women in childbirth. But with the institutionalisation of childbirth, women have lost control over many decisions concerning their bodies. It was this dialectic that came to the foreground in our show.

Starting with educational need: Telegraph Hill School

In Summer 2000 I ran a playwriting project at Telegraph Hill School in Lewisham, London with writer Lisa Levi. This presented us with challenges we'd rarely experienced. Pupil numbers were declining dramatically, absenteeism was rife and the majority of those who did attend displayed severe emotional and behavioural problems.

During the second session, a girl approaches us and tells us with elation she won't be with us for our next session.

'I'm leaving! I'm going to Deptford Green on Monday!'

Her colleagues jeer. A look of resignation falls on all the faces. She's lucky. She's escaped.

In many ways, this short exchange epitomises the collective low self-esteem of the group. Concentration spans are extremely short, those who do attend are often very late and bullying is endemic. Many tasks are left unfinished – sabotaged by challenging behaviour, abandoned in order to make way for another initiative or forgotten when the timetable is re-organised.

When Kate Page, the Head of Expressive Arts, invited us to run this residency with a year 9 group, she briefed us on the problems we might face, adding that the average reading age in this secondary school is eight. Telegraph Hill is a new name, part of a 'fresh start' initiative. There is a new head teacher, many new members of staff and an ethos that embraces the arts – and particularly drama – as a way to help turn the school around.

Within this context, Lisa and I have four days over a month to create some script with the young people. On a fifth day we plan to bring professional actors into the school and present an animated reading.

Developing literacy is clearly an underlying purpose of the project. However, in many ways, citizenship is the hidden engine at its heart. These two areas of the curriculum are inextricably connected – how can anyone play a full democratic part in their community if their basic skills are inadequate? And there is another aim: the class are poor at group-work and it is hoped that this project will help equip them to negotiate with others and – through their writing – present an articulate depiction of the issues they face every day.

I've always thought one should start making theatre from what we know, as we're all experts in our own lives. Lisa and I instinctively realise that these young people, despite their jaded and distracted manner, might become motivated if their worldview is validated. If we are to encourage them to write, then we should emphasise their role as authors – giving them responsibility and control over the meaning of our play. It's also important to make it clear that we aren't concerned with spelling, grammar and neatness, so as to avoid a potential trigger for disruption.

We realise our group has, ironically, a collective 'losing script'. Each day mirrors the shape of a tragic narrative – moving towards a predictable finale where a violent incident leaves pupils facing disciplinary action. Disappointing themselves and their teachers is the common pattern in every lesson. Psychologically, this is comfortable for the group. Finishing the play is going to mean changing this group's self-perception completely – motivating them to transform themselves into a group with a winning script.

We decide to emphasise our roles as artists rather than teachers: Lisa as playwright and myself as director. We want to avoid the trap of being too non-directive; of giving the group a coded message that we are detached professionals who don't care. All our actions demonstrate the investment of our own creativity into the work. Utterances of characters, pace of scenes and the arc of the narrative all matter deeply to us as artists. And this way of working also distinguishes us in the eyes of our pupils as special and distinct from the other peripatetic workers in the school, such as supply teachers.

In previous writing residencies we tried to maintain a specific integrity, creating short plays that were wholly the products of the pupils' endeavours. In this instance it's clear that the group are highly unlikely to complete such a task in the allotted time and that their pattern of low achievement will probably be repeated. These factors dictate the shape of the project. We decide to limit our ambition to one play collectively created, with a significant writing input from Lisa. We know we will have to work hard between the sessions, writing and refining the play in order to give the group a sense of accomplishment through their collaboration with professional artists.

Our first session focuses on the notion of 'artistic truth'. Many people who have tried to write plays with young people will be familiar with seeing them regurgitate film and TV dramas. We all learn instinctively about the shape of a story from our own consumption of books, TV, film and oral storytelling. It's understandable that young people will use their favourite TV shows and films as a template for their own writing, a failing compounded by a school system that implicitly discourages originality and creativity. Each pupil knows they're assessed chiefly according to a display of technical competence and they're seldom truly encouraged to express their feelings and opinions. After all, feelings can't be marked as correct or incorrect and they may be uncomfortable for a teacher to handle. Drama classes – and to a lesser extent the other arts – are frequently the only times in the curriculum where a fairly direct expression of feeling is actively encouraged. In other lessons young people's dominant experience is to be rewarded for 'good behaviour' – silence, compliance and obedience.

Given the ubiquity of American TV and film I begin by asking the group:

> 'Can you put your hand up if you've ever experienced a Los Angeles police department at first hand?'

This is greeted by silence.

> 'OK. Who here has ever shared a flat with friends in Manhattan?'

Silence again. Of course, no one in the class can write or speak about these environments with authenticity.

> 'We'd need to do a lot of research to understand an environment we don't know at all. And we don't have enough time. Let's start this play by writing about what we know, telling our unique stories to our audience.'

So we start with a game to demonstrate the connection between artistic truth and real facts. Each player is invited to say three things about themselves. Two have to be true and one a lie. The aim of the game is to mask the lie by trying to make it sound as realistic as possible.

> 'I didn't have no breakfast this morning, my cousin's Eddie Murphy and I've got two sisters.'

The class erupts with laughter. This is too obvious.

> 'She ain't related to Eddie Murphy!'

> 'Is that right?' I ask.

> 'Yeah'

A young man offers his facts.

> 'I live in Evesham Road, my mum's name is Tracy and I've got one sister and a half brother.'

This proves more difficult. The class is evenly split in terms of spotting the lie. The boy admits he really lives in Evesham *Road.* Everyone laughs and then someone points out:

'Yeah, but all those facts are boring. Couldn't you have found anything more interesting?'

So we talk about how our play can be dramatic *and* believable. The next contribution sets the tone.

'I've just moved house, I live next door to a mental hospital and a bloke got shot down my street last week.'

After much discussion, it transpires that the second fact is the lie. The most extreme statement – that someone was shot – is, sadly, the truth. We discuss this. Yes, dramatic things happen, but not in the way that they occur in American action films. This is one shooting. Yes, we could use it as content for our play, but let's be careful about adding more shootings, a car chase and a multinational drugs deal. The appeal to be believable is connecting with this group. After all, they are a cynical and highly critical audience themselves.

Now we were in a position to start creating our own believable characters. In small groups of two or three, the class draws the outline of a body. This will be a character in our play. The head is the place where thinking happens. This can be represented by a motto. We talk about what kind of mottoes – or driving belief systems – people might live by:

'God will guide me.'

'He who lives by the sword....'

'It's the law of the jungle out there.'

'Do unto others....'

The groups pick one motto at random and write it on each character's head.

We move to the heart – the place where feeling happens. Each group writes the strongest emotion or passion of their character next to the heart of their outlined body. Already the class cannot resist creating fragments of narrative.

'He's a really jealous person. He wants this girl....'

'She just wants respect. But this boy treats her as his possession.'

And we start to see how authentic experiences are starting to be channelled through our emerging fiction.

Other details are filled into the body outline. One hand represents the character's greatest skills and talents; the other their challenges and weaknesses. One leg represents how they see their future; the other, an important incident from the character's past. Finally, they give their character a name and list any other details that have emerged from the exercise: a job; family connections; how old they are.

The characters have now taken on a fuller and more interesting life. The groups create a spider diagram with their character at the centre. The character is now linked to other important people in their lives. The lines connecting the characters represent the nature of each relationship – the feelings and the history.

Lisa has a look at the emerging list of characters. She comments that the choice of names (Tairique, Sharnai etc) are either taken from or influenced by American teen sitcoms. And there was I thinking we had tapped a source of originality! Despite this, the group is getting nearer to expressing something in their own voice.

It will be a week until the next session. Lisa works hard to create a coherent plot incorporating elements from every group's work. Somehow, she achieves this. A school-based story emerges centring on boy/girl twins (a popular theme with the group) and a love triangle between the girl, a new boy and a degenerate ex-pupil. Lisa prepares a scene-by-scene structure to show to the group. Each scene is titled and has a beginning. Their job will be to continue each scene.

The following session has mixed success. When he sees there will be a writing task, one young man excuses himself to the toilet and disappears for the rest of the day. Others rebel in a variety of ways – drawing cartoons (although this is related to the task in hand), chatting in corners and pulling chairs away from under each other. We do, however, come away from the session with some progress made. Portions of dialogue have been generated. One group even refines Lisa's plot, adding in a Restoration-style love-letter mix up.

The following two sessions are a mixture of games, improvisation and writing exercises. Memorably, the most disruptive pupil – on the edge of expulsion from the school – relishes the opportunity to play the villain of the piece, Tairique, in an extended improvisation. This is the climactic scene of our play, where Tairique – a seventeen-year-old who left the school the previous year – bursts into a classroom to confront Sharnai and her new boyfriend. He terrorises the class with a knife. It's both fascinating and unnerving to observe the absorption in-role of a young person playing his potential future self. No explicit connection is made between actor and part. The team has agreed that this character is 'sad', that school has left him ill-prepared for adulthood and that his future prospects are bleak. Lisa and I are left wondering if this actor is destined to become his part? Or will this project affect his prospects in some way?

By our final session Lisa has completed a half-hour play including as many ideas from the group as she can. We spend a day creating a rehearsed reading of the play with a group of five professional actors. The actors are chosen not just for their ability to play the parts but also for their sensitivity to our context and to reflect the multicultural nature of our writing group and audience.

The actors meet their writers to a mixed response:

'Haven't you learned it?'

'Ain'tcha got no costumes?'

'You been on the telly?'

The class watches a run through of the play and their wariness drops away. Here are confident readers who are breathing life into their script. Here are impressively skilled professional actors and maybe they've been to schools like Telegraph Hill and have overcome difficult circumstances to take their place in a highly competitive profession. That they are reading from scripts turns out to be a bonus. The sheaf of papers in their hands is the work of this class, the physical evidence of an unusual phenomenon – a group task completed.

The final event of the residency is the presentation of the play to the rest of Year 9. It is then that Lisa and I feel a sense of accomplishment. The play grips and moves the audience – even as a rehearsed reading – more than most profes-sionally written plays can engage an audience of this kind. It reflects back their experience, their school and their own language. The audience is noisy. Those watching the play cheer, boo the villain and comment constantly to their neigh-bours. Those who had been part of the writing team glow with pride. They turn to friends and claim lines, character names and plot-twists as their own creations. The ovation at the end is sincere and passionate.

To give shape to my experiences, I've admittedly edited this story to try to create a structure that might engage my own audience/readership. I've shifted some of the more frustrating incidents into the background, such as the extraordinary amount of time we wasted trying to get the group to settle at the beginning of the session; the times when they let us know how boring they thought we were. And, just as the young people we were working with were constantly fictionalis-ing their real lives in juxtaposition to the popular media, I was fantasising about being a Hollywood-movie teacher – a Robin Williams or Sidney Poitier – in-spiring the class with a life-transforming experience. The truth is more complex than that.

Despite the undoubtedly positive impact of the final event, the head teacher left the school shortly after our residency. The regime that encouraged positive re-enforcement, gentleness and creativity would be replaced with a less liberal management. The experiment had failed and the drama budget would be cut. I have now learned that the school will be closed and the children dispersed around the borough.

In a short time we had made an impact on the lives of these young people. We had given them an alternative future to imagine – a glimpse of a 'winning script'. Maybe their life stories won't end with them as the perpetrators or victims of crime. Maybe they won't have a lifetime of struggling with poorly paid jobs and reliance on state benefits. Maybe they will play an active part as citizens in their communities.

If every child in the country were to be entitled to these experiences on a regular basis there would naturally be financial implications. But if education doesn't change radically, what will the social costs be? Shouldn't we be civilised enough to aspire to virtually empty our prisons over a generation and thus save enormous costs to the state in the long run? Indeed, current schemes such as the DCMS' Creative Partnerships seem to be addressing the deficit. But perhaps the hardest change to make will be the ideological shift from a mechanistic to a creative pedagogy.

So, let us dream. Let us write a winning political script. Let us imagine that creative education is not a rarity, but that it has become enshrined to underpin the core curriculum entitlement of every child. Let us look to twenty years in the future. Then we'll have to face the inevitable dilemma inherent in having a population educated to be literate, articulate and active citizens. Who'll be left to serve the burgers?

Starting with self: research workshops for *One Thursday*

The play *One Thursday* was designed by three professional actor/teachers for performance to young people in schools and youth centres. We wanted the dialogue and narrative details to be as authentic as possible so we undertook one-off devising workshops with young people. We felt we needed this contact to create a play with an authentic feel to the dialogue and details of narrative. The success or otherwise of this venture can, in part, be judged by reading the play, reproduced here as chapter four.

One strand of the play, Femi's story, had a particularly fascinating genesis – in the real experiences of several of the young people. The team started by asking the Theatre Royal's Senior Youth Theatre to tell stories about occasions when they had encountered barriers to achieving their personal goals. Two scenes had particularly high recognition value for their our future audiences:

- Ysanne depicted the dilemma for a black family living in a tough inner-city area. Her mother constantly berated her for 'mixing with the wrong sort' – in other words the group of black young people hanging about in the street. Despite Ysanne's protestations that her friends were honest and loyal, her mother asked her not to befriend them. It wasn't that the kids were bad, it was just that they were bound to get into trouble with the police. Sure enough, the police stop and question the group as mother is watching from her window. It confirms her worst suspicions – the racism of the police means that her daughter will get into trouble – guilt by association. Ysanne gets grounded and argues over the injustice.

- Meanwhile, another group was staging their own version of conflicts with the police. This time the protagonist is Djan – a Turkish Cypriot young man who identifies strongly with black/hip-hop culture. His story describes the day to day stop and search and questioning he gets from the police, even though there is no evidence of any wrong-doing.

Back on the rehearsal floor our team discusses the material that has emerged. I'm cautious about working up a story about police harassment and young black men. How can we tell the story truthfully, without lapsing into cliché?, One of our actors, Antonia, contributes her own experiences. She too was arrested by racist police officers when she was younger. She describes how the police bundled her into a car when they questioned her. When she asked what her crime was, she was told: 'you've failed the attitude test'. This was a powerful testament, made all the stronger when she revealed that she hadn't recognised the irony in the police officer's words and thought there really was an attitude test!

We decided to devise a scene combining elements of Ysanne, Djan and Antonia's stories. Concerned that Antonia's experiences might be dated, having happened over ten years ago, we took our model scenes in rough form back to our group. The narrative that had now become Femi's story was improvised in front of the group. To our relief, this not uncritical group of young people confirmed that we had pulled together a story that rang true for the young people of East London.

We were both saddened and spurred on by the fact that the disrespect shown by the police to 'Femi' was recognised as a universal truth by an alarmingly large number of young people who witnessed the show. We decided to depict the police officer's racism as subtextual and indirect, with the knowledge that direct and abusive racism was (and is still) not an uncommon experience either. It fell to the actor to know the attitude behind, for example, the mispronunciation of Femi's surname – Adewole – using an inflection that betrayed the policeman's own attitude. Interestingly, Femi's story resonated with young people from a whole variety of backgrounds. Young white and Asian people recognised their experiences in the story and, on one notable occasion a group of young white women told of their run-ins with prejudiced police officers during the after-show discussion.

The strength of this method lay, in large measure, in the team of devising actors who had skill, integrity and experiences of their own of growing up in the inner-city. That is not to say that this method can't be replicated with groups new to acting. The very act of translating real experiences into engaging theatre enables each player to reflect on the social dynamics in a way that excites understanding.

One thing all these examples of real practice show clearly is that: choosing a good starting point gives great impetus to making a play and it is vital that it chimes with the group's social and cultural enthusiasms.

8
Youth Parliaments and Forums:
a model

Augusto Boal, the great Brazilian theatre practitioner, was elected as a local councillor for Rio de Janeiro for four years in 1992. In his book *Legislative Theatre* (1998) he describes how he promulgated thirteen bills that became municipal laws by using the techniques of Theatre of the Oppressed. Since that time, a number of theatre workers interested in engaging with the political process have sought to replicate and modify Boal's ground-breaking work in their own contexts throughout the world.

Boal's work gains new significance with the advent of citizenship initiatives for young people in the UK. For many young people, teachers, youth workers and community activists the ethos and methods of the work make sense. Drama inherently encourages effective and democratic ways of understanding the world we inhabit, exploring the power structures that influence us and, crucially, enabling us to present our own ways forward.

Inevitably, there is a tension between this *participatory* form of democratic expression and the *representative* democracy that is enshrined in our current voting system. The Citizenship curriculum and other parallel initiatives seek to involve young people as a way to counteract the perceived apathy and alienation to the present system. But increased levels of activism by young people will not necessarily produce higher levels of voter turnout if politicians are unwilling to listen and respond to the newly expressed points of view of their young constituents.

The model of work proposed in this chapter – the youth conference – is a bottom-up approach that fundamentally challenges some of the foundations of the current system. The culture of our democracy can produce powerful psychological barriers to participation – with many citizens, young and old, experiencing little ongoing accountability. Young people especially feel that they are somehow accountable to the state. Their dealings with, say, schools, hospitals, social services and the police are often perceived as battles with monolithic institutions to whom *they* must be accountable. In addition, in a variety of direct and indirect ways, the message is clearly sent out that you need to be an expert to presume to propose changes in policy and legislation. The irony of increasing avenues for genuine participation is that it won't increase voter turnout amongst the young if the exercise is perceived as cynical, cosmetic and a strategy for containment.

I hope that this simple and effective model of work will be adapted in contexts where a genuine dialogue is desired between young people and the people who make the rules under which they live. The development of a local, regional or national youth parliament, a school parliament or any other forum on key issues can benefit from this approach. Although one may remain cynical about key issues of sustainability and containment, perhaps it is only by disseminating and engaging with models such as the youth conference that the extent of the state's accountability can be tested.

An experiment in Tower Hamlets

It was the end of a gruelling two-day youth conference in the relatively plush surroundings of London's County Hall. The irony that this erstwhile home to a vibrant and popular local democracy was now a conference centre and hotel was not lost on the older people at the conference but the younger ones knew nothing about building's previous purpose.

Politicians had been invited to attend the forum presented by the young people of Tower Hamlets. Of the four MPs who said they would attend, only one non-local MP turned up. Local councillors were in greater evidence, an MEP sent a deputy and one councillor of the newly created Greater London Authority was present.

The young people presented scenes depicting the real problems they faced and their own ideas for ways forward. It was revealed, for example, that 80% of lessons were perceived as old-fashioned 'chalk and talk' classes. Teaching of this kind was shown as the trigger for a fictional class to behave badly. A companion scene showed a teacher engaging with the story of the French Revolution, drawing in the students by interesting them in the guillotine as spectacle. Why, the young people asked the politicians, could they not campaign for better quality training for teachers, since more interesting classes would prevent behavioural problems borne from boredom?

Following an open forum, the theatre work triggered genuine dialogue between the young people and those in power. The Greater London Authority councillor, active on the Metropolitan Police Committee, tussled with a group of

Bangladeshi young men who had experienced racial taunts from police over the problem of recruiting ethnic minority people into the police. Another local councillor became aware for the first time of the extent of teenage prostitution and committed herself to further exploration of the issue.

But perhaps the major benefit of the workshop was the exchange between young people from very different backgrounds who share the same turf. In Tower Hamlets, tensions are often keenly felt across racial groups and different geographical groupings. By the end of the two days, there was a sense that the young people taking part were motivated, working as a team and able to speak powerfully for young people. The big question still remaining is whether workers on the ground can sustain the positive initial momentum.

The youth conference model described

The following workshop plan has developed from the work with Tower Hamlets LEA and others. The conference requires two days if undertaken in its entirety for a group of up to thirty young people. It also requires detailed preparatory work and development work following up the initial impetus. The main objective of the workshop is to initiate or refresh a youth forum as an active body that engages with those responsible for making policy and regulation. It also aims to provide a high quality learning experience, easily adaptable for use by teachers, youth workers and others, and flexible enough to cope with the constraints of time and resources.

As in the case of Tower Hamlets, the premise is to work intensively with one group. Its members should be carefully selected to be representative of the gender, cultural, class and geographic character of the constituency. It's also important to acknowledge that only young people with particular motivation are likely to participate willingly and usefully. In this sense, the workshop can be seen as an exercise in developing leadership and that more young people will become involved as a result of the workshop. So it is vital to recruit with care. Those responsible for selecting participants should be aware that many leadership qualities such as articulacy, listening, negotiation and vision are not necessarily consistent with high academic achievement or popularity with teachers and group-leaders. To this end an election within each class or constituency – supported by an open discussion on leadership qualities – might best produce a motivated and representative group. In addition, as part of an ongoing citizenship programme, it's crucial that the conference establishes a solid platform for ongoing work.

The model described is an ideal. Understandably, day to day constraints can make the organisation of a project of this nature seem impossible. The scheme of work described here can be adapted to a variety of circumstances. However, it's worth considering that the two-day model is highly desirable, particularly if the two days are consecutive. This adds considerable momentum and focus to the event. It could be argued that an institution or organisation that's unwilling to support a modest two day conference for a select group of young people is not really serious about participation and citizenship.

The basis for all the drama work is the re-telling of true stories. Naturally, this provides a powerful incentive for those taking part. Group-leaders should be aware that many of the exercises suggested below are designed to connect the particular experiences related in the stories to the universal questions of rights and responsibilities and then to practical steps to create positive change. As this process is at the heart of the conference, it may be difficult to adapt it to explore concerns at a distance from young people's experience, such as matters affecting the poorer countries of the world. However, I do believe that this model of work is adaptable. In the case of development issues, for example, group-leaders can draw connections to real experiences of, say, consumer culture or immigration.

Advance preparation

1. A suitable venue is located. Ideally, this should facilitate small group work as well as providing a sizeable space for plenary/forum sessions. The venue should also be well-equipped with presentation resources such as flip charts and overhead projectors.

2. A mailing list of people of influence is collated, to include all elected politicians for the locality and relevant policy makers such as the Head of Youth Service. Everyone should receive an invitation to the final forum event at the end, briefly outlining the purpose of the occasion. It might also be useful to invite local press and radio, as yet another carrot to entice the people who have power.

3. If the agenda is pre-set, key speakers could be invited to contribute briefly. Select these speakers with caution, as a speaker who bores or frustrates the participants will severely hamper the creative work. Make sure they are briefed about the desired content and especially the time allocated for their talk.

4. A representative group of young people should be recruited as conference 'delegates'. If elections are impractical, then group-leaders should be careful to ensure that diverse voices are heard, giving particular attention to marginalised groups.

5. Where possible, the conference delegates should elicit agenda items from their constituents. For example, if the conference is to be used to set up a school parliament, a student from each class could lead a brainstorming session a few days before the conference.

6. Staff should be thoroughly briefed in terms of preparing the group for the sessions, emphasising their roles and setting up sustainable follow-up activity.

Day one – morning session

1. An introduction clearly outlines the aims and activities for the next two days. The main objective is defined: to produce effective presentations for the invited people of influence at the final forum event.

2. Group-bonding games and exercises. These should be designed to establish the ethos of the conference, particularly in ensuring that players are aware of the need to share involvement as fairly and equally as possible. Chapter three suggests appropriate strategies for doing this.

3. Four small groups of players brainstorm 'something should be done about....' The only limitation on this task is that each response should be relevant to the players' own community. Any themes from the pre-work are brought forward.

4. Following the brainstorm, each group discusses real instances in their experience where they felt that particular agenda item strongly. From these fragments of narrative each foursome creates three still images to depict the three hottest topics.

5. The images are presented and discussed by the whole group. During the discussion, the group-leader reflects back which topics seem either most popular or most passionately felt. Because of the time constraints of a two-day conference, not all issues can be dealt with.

6. Back in the foursomes, the agenda is whittled down to one area for each group that they see as of urgent concern. The group-leaders ensure each group works on a different topic. The choice of topic should reflect the extent or severity of the problem, the strong feelings it arouses and the prospects for action in the light of the influential people who will be attending the final session.

7. Starting with the initial image of the problem, each foursome creates an improvised scene depicting an authentic incident that epitomises the issue under scrutiny. Some of the techniques described in previous chapters can be adapted for this purpose.

8. The first session ends with sharing and discussing these pieces, the whole group checking them for authenticity and theatrical power. The pieces will be worked on again, so allowing other players to interject and suggest added detail drawn from their own experience.

Day one – afternoon session

1. Each player chooses one of the four topics on the agenda that affects them most strongly. They find a partner outside their own foursome and take turns to practice presenting the problem as persuasively as possible to one another. The listening partner gives feedback on the effectiveness of the other's presentation.

2. The persuasion exercise is then repeated in a number of different ways to evoke possible responses from those with the power to bring about change. The pair themselves start by deciding who they would wish to confront with the issue – a local or national politician, perhaps, or a headteacher or the local chief constable. There follows a series of role-plays:

   • The influential person (IP) is rushing to an important meeting. You manage to get hold of them hurrying down a corridor. Can you persuade them to stop and listen to you?

   • The IP shows that they completely disagree with you. Can you shift them towards your point of view?

   • The IP tries to shift the responsibility to someone else. Can you get them to take any responsibility?

   • The IP seems to agree with you in principle, and tries to make you understand the practical hurdles to making changes (i.e. insufficient money). Can you still get them to act?

   A spirit of playfulness should be encouraged in the role-plays. Those playing the IPs should try to set up challenges for their partners, without blocking off all their options. To ensure this, how the improvisation is set-up is important. Group-leaders might find it useful to prompt each pair to set up the location, time and other details for the role-plays carefully so as to build a strong sense of belief in the various scenarios.

3. As a reflection exercise, two pairs create a group of four and discuss their findings. In which of the role-plays did they make most headway? Which was the most frustrating? Which arguments or strategies worked best? What tactics were the least effective? How do you imagine the exercise compares to the reality of communicating with people who have influence and power?

4. All the delegates gather together and write up on a chart the arguments and tactics they rated as effective and ineffective. For example, how important is courtesy and keeping your cool? Did anyone manage to get their IP to commit to any action? If so, how?

5. A group-leader introduces the notions of *lobbying* and *campaigning*. The origins of both words are worth discussing. The word *lobby* derives from the practice of frequenting the lobby of a legislative assembly or parliament with the intention of influencing the members' votes. In a sense, this implies that an IP can themselves be influenced and that their inaction on the issue might be due to their regarding it as a low priority. *Campaigning*, on the other hand, originates in a military context and implies the gathering together of forces to overwhelm the opposition. The role-play exercise explored the concept of lobbying – including the valuable lesson that it might well be a waste of time to lobby someone totally opposed to your own position. When we think of campaigning, the difficulty is converting passive support to active participation.

6. As an exercise in exploring campaigning, each foursome reconvenes to decide on a concrete objective that relates to the problem they're exploring. Then they make a list of the people they might lobby and those who might join a campaign.

    For example:

PROBLEM	OBJECTIVE	TO LOBBY	CAMPAIGN SUPPORT
Nowhere for young people to go in their spare time.	Create a new leisure centre for the area.	Local council. MP.	Other young people. Parents. Teachers. Police. Youth Workers.

8. The foursome quickly makes a list of the reasons why people might be reluctant to join a campaign: for example apathy, lack of time or the view that it will involve lots of boring meetings. They decide on a suitable campaign strategy – a petition, a festival or a letter-writing campaign, for example. They can now role-play in pairs, trying to persuade their partner to get involved with the campaign.

9. Time is allocated for reflection on the relationship between lobbying and campaigning, relating it to their own specific agenda. Would it be useful to take time to gather greater support? How broad should that support be?

What kind of campaign might make the best lobby (i.e. something that will gain the attention and sympathy of IPs)? Have they got a clear objective?

Day two – morning session

1. The session starts with more drama games, designed to prepare the group for improvisation and presentation work.

2. The original scenes depicting the problem are viewed again. This time, a group-leader asks the gathering how the situation might be improved – particularly in the light of the specific campaign objectives revealed at the end of day one.

3. The improvements are added to the scene in an 'as if perfect' scenario. For example:

    • A scene of youth boredom is replayed to show a youth worker opening the doors to a new leisure centre.

    • A potential mugging outside a school is stopped by a group of volunteer 'guardian angels'.

    • School facilities are opened up evenings and weekends to support homework.

4. Following a showing of these dream scenarios, the gathering are asked to add a 'hazard', to show how matters could go wrong in the real world.

    • The cost of the new leisure centre is prohibitive.

    • The muggers wait for their chance around the corner, out of sight of the school gates.

    • Homework facilities are only made available at the most academic school.

5. Considering their findings, each foursome refines a scene to show a *realistic improvement* to their original problem.

6. The realistic improvement scene is then juxtaposed to the original problem scene, ready for presentation to the IPs that afternoon. Each foursome should also work on creating explicit links or statements so that the presentation has smoothness and clarity.

7. Before lunch, the gathering is briefed on the final session – particularly the small group work with the IPs. Each group is given a flip-chart to record any commitment to action the IPs might make.

Day two – afternoon session

1. The session to which IPs are invited lasts approximately an hour and a half. Following a brief introduction, outlining what has gone on in the conference so far, each group makes their presentation.

2. Following each scene, the IPs are asked to comment on the improvements it puts forward. A hand count should be made of the IPs who are broadly in favour of the proposals.

3. After all the presentations, the IPs are invited to join the small group which most closely matches their particular interest. The aim is to record any action that the IPs are willing to undertake as a result of the session, and to establish agreement on a realistic timescale (e.g. Councillor Bloggs to table a motion to the Education Committee within three months).

4. The IPs are thanked for their participation and encouraged to follow their commitments through.

5. Each action plan is reviewed and discussed by all the young people together. Are the promises from the IPs firm? Do they go far enough?

6. To conclude the conference, the young people work on legacy strategies to keep up the pressure. This might include:

   • Delegating specific people to follow up items on the action plans.

   • Setting dates for sessions in the next twelve months. It may be helpful for the group-leaders to provide proforma calendars.

   • Setting up processes to involve other young people. This can hark back to the session on campaigning and might, for example, include setting up a petition or letter-writing campaign.

   • Looking at other activities for the group to keep up momentum, such as a residential weekend or an outing. Group-leaders should be aware that social factors are central to sustaining young people in a vibrant group. There may be events relating to the key issues discussed at the conference, such as plays and films on a specific topic or a visit to the spectators' gallery at the House of Commons or local council. However, even unrelated and seemingly recreational events can help keep the group together.

How can the model be developed?

So far, this model has proved effective as a one-off event, being used by Tower Hamlets Council as part of its strategy to create a stronger voice for young people. However, there is no evidence as yet that concrete change has occurred as a result. This is a good idea that, despite evidence of effectiveness of the Legislative Theatre as used by Boal in Brazil, needs more time and resources devoted to it in the UK to test it thoroughly. The two key challenges are the sustainability of the model and its replication in new contexts.

It's worth outlining some of the potential barriers to sustaining this model and positing some ways of producing an endurable youth forum/parliament.

The process of political activism can be extremely frustrating for young people used to instant gratification from their other extra-curricular activities. So, as with many youth groups, maintaining commitment is key. In addition to the social bonding that can be encouraged, it's important that players are also engaged with the main purpose of the group – and this can be a bigger challenge. Effecting real change can be very motivating and ultimately important if participatory democracy is going to mean anything, but it's vital that results are achieved as quickly as possible. Consequently, it's worth appraising objectives realistically in terms of their chances of success: for example, it may be easier to obtain, say, youth representation as a regular feature of council business than to get a new school built. That is not to say that more ambitious campaigns should not be pursued, but it's important to recognise that momentum can flounder. So the buzz of creating events – fundraisers, media events and imaginative protests – can provide interim motivation, while the larger objective is always kept in mind.

Note also that sustainability depends on the good will and effectiveness of key workers such as youth workers and teachers. Citizenship initiatives are too often just one of several competing demands in a stressful workload. It's therefore paramount that the leadership in institutions demonstrates the high priority given to citizenship initiatives by supporting key workers. In practice, this means giving practical recognition of the time spent on a project by arranging cover and factoring in professional development opportunities.

Young people will want to move on or get interested in other activities as they grow older, so it's reasonable to expect a yearly turnover of participants. It's therefore essential to take care that those initiating the youth parliament or forum, along with the key workers, demonstrate an open attitude that encourages new people to come in.

There is already a growing network in the UK of school and youth parliaments with a regional and national structure. Many youth services and schools are already tapped into these organisations and are promoting activities for greater involvement.

There is, however, little understanding of drama as a methodology to support the grass roots work. As I hope will be apparent from the description of the conference, the drama strategies can be employed by a range of workers as long as they have the confidence to try them out. But one shouldn't underestimate the value of specialist drama workers in creating an event. Professional performers are often excellent role models as effective communicators and their experience will be of inestimable value to young people in understanding the dynamics of performance, particularly language, space and interactivity. Given the current political climate, there is every chance that a local authority will provide the funds for such an event, which will have the added bonus of giving it extra status too.

Consequently, the use of drama specialists up and down the country could be key to the expansion of the model. Here we hit upon a problem, in terms of the quantity and quality of expertise available. There are many people with the relevant expertise and a telephone call to the local theatre's education personnel or to a local TIE (Theatre-in-Education) company may well secure appropriate workers. But with the drastic reduction of this work over the eighties and nineties, it's harder to find good people. A training infrastructure is therefore required if this and similar models of practice are to be replicated. Clearly, 'joined up thinking' becomes important. Imaginative schemes of work such as this model can be realised if those responsible for national policy in the arts, education and training work together to provide straightforward access to the necessary resources.

Meanwhile, it's not always essential that those on the ground wait for the state to recognise models of good practice before involving themselves. Drama work has the advantage of being relatively adaptable, 'low-tech' and instant. I hope that this book will encourage teachers, drama workers, youth workers and others involved in community development to make their own connections and start using drama for citizenship today.

Bibliography

Allen, D. and Fallow, J (1998) *Stanislavski for Beginners* Writers and Readers

Boal, A. (1979) *Theatre of the Oppressed* Pluto Press

Boal, A. (1998) *Legislative Theatre* Routledge

Boal, A. (1995) *The Rainbow of Desire* Routledge

Boal, A. (1992) *Games For Actors and Non-Actors* Routledge

Courtney, R. (1989) *Play, Drama and Thought* Simon and Pierre Publishing, Toronto

Bolton, G. (1984) *Drama as Education* Longman

Bolton, G. (1986) *Selected Writings* Longman

Crick, B. *et al* (1998) *Education for Citizenship and the Teaching of Democracy in Schools* Qualifications and Curriculum Authority.

Garlake T. and Pocock M. (2000) *Partners in Rights: creative activities exploring rights and citizenship* Save the Children

Hannam, D. (2001) *Pupil Voice and Democracy* Department for Education and Skills

Heathcote, D. (1984) *Collected Writings on Education and Drama* Hutchinson

Hertz, N. (2001) *It's Not About Apathy* Guardian Unlimited – www.guardian.co.uk

Hevey, D. (1992) *The Creatures Time Forgot: photography and disability imagery* Routledge

Johnston, C. (1998) *House of Games: making theatre from everyday life* Nick Hern Books

Hunt, A. (1977) *Hopes For Great Happenings* Tapplinger Publishing Co

Ikoli, T. (1998) *Scrape Off The Black* Oberon Books

Jackson, T. (Ed) (1993) *Learning Through Theatre: new perspectives on theatre in education* Routledge

Johnstone, K (1981) *Impro: improvisation and the theatre* Methuen

Johnson, V. *et al* (1998) *Stepping Forward: children and young people's participation in the development process* Intermediate Technology Publications

Littlewood, J. (1994) *Joan's Book: Joan Littlewood's peculiar history as she tells it* Methuen

Macbeth, F. and Fine, N. (1995) *Playing with Fire: creative conflict resolution for young adults* New Society Publishers

Neelands, J. (1990) *Structuring Drama Work: a handbook of available forms in theatre and drama* Cambridge University Press

O'Neill C. and Lambert A. (1982) *Drama Structures: A practical handbook for teachers* Stanley Thornes Ltd

Paley, V. G. (1990) *The Boy who Would be a Helicopter* Harvard University Press

Poulter, C. (1987) *Playing the Game* Macmillan

Putnam, R. (2000) *Bowling Alone: the collapse and revival of American community* Simon and Schuster

Stanislavski, C. (1979) *Building a Character* Methuen

Spolin, V. (1963) *Improvisation For The Theatre* Northwestern University Press

Theatre Workshop. (1974) *Oh What a Lovely War* Eyre Methuen

Wagner, B.J. (1980) *Dorothy Heathcote: drama as a learning medium* Stanley Thornes

Williams, R. (1999) *Starstruck/The No Boys Cricket Club* Methuen

Useful websites with links to other sites

Citizenship Foundation: www.citfou.org.uk

Common Purpose: www.citizensconnection.net

Arts Council of England: www.artscouncil.org.uk

The Citizenship Foundation

The Citizenship Foundation supports and promotes citizenship education in schools, youth organisations, community groups, local councils and international links. Based in London, CF works throughout the UK, offering advice, training and resources. In addition, the Citizenship Foundation organises two mock trial competitions and a youth parliament competition. There is a twinning scheme which matches trainee solicitors with schools to teach aspects of the law, and a national Speakers in Schools project which brings barristers to school to discuss human rights issues. CF works in partnership with a variety of organisations such as the Institute for Global Ethics, running a Citizenship Values Awards scheme for schools and youth organisations.

CF identifies and disseminates examples of useful contacts and good practice in citizenship education via its website, newsletter and courses. You can contact the Citizenship Foundation at:

Ferroners House
Shaftesbury Place
Off Aldersgate St
London EC2Y 8AA
Tel. 020 7367 0500
Email: info@citfou.org.uk
www.citfou.org.uk

Published materials include:

Introducing Citizenship: a practical handbook and video for primary schools
by Don Rowe, published by A & C Black
Handbook and video – ISBN: 0-713-65857-6; price: £14.99
Order from A & C Black, PO Box 19, St Neots, Cambs PE19 8SF; 01480 212666; sales@acblack.com

You, Me, Us!
by Don Rowe and Jan Newton
This folder of specially written stories and exercises introduces primary school children to many key citizenship concepts.
To order (2 free copies per school): Tel 0870 241 4680; Fax 0870 241 4786; or write to: Prolog (Home Office Publications), Sherwood Park, Annesley, Notts NG15 0BR.

Citizenship for All
edited by Don Rowe, published by Nelson Thornes
A wide-ability resource book covering many personal and social issues.
Tel. 01242 267100. Price £40. ISBN 0-7487-3196-2.

Citizenship Studies
published by Hodder and Stoughton (in press)
A textbook to support the OCR examination board's GCSE short course in Citizenship.

Good Thinking: Education for Citizenship and Moral Responsibility
by Ted Huddleston and Don Rowe, published by Evans Education
Three courses of study for Key Stages 3, 4 and '5', introducing students to moral ideas, language and debate, within a framework of citizenship and public morality.
£20 each. Orders can be emailed to sales@evansbooks.co.uk, or faxed on 020 7487 0921.

Passport to Life
published by United Response
A new guide to the law specifically for people with disabilities.
£7 – individuals and citizen advocates; £12 – organisations
Email purchase: passport@united-response.co.uk
Fax purchase: 01347 823 242
Postal purchase (please include a cheque payable to 'Lantern Trading'): The Old Boot Shop, Chapel Lane, Easingwood, York Y06 3AE

Changing Places
by Ted Huddleston, published by the National Youth Agency
A practical handbook for active citizenship and community involvement.
Price £3.95 Available from the NYA Tel: 0116 285 3709; Fax: 0116 285 3777
Email: sales@nya.org.uk.

Understanding Citizenship
by Tony Thorpe, published by Hodder and Stoughton
A progressive course (3 students' books and Teachers' Book) for Key Stage 3

Young Citizen's Passport – Citizenship Edition
edited by Tony Thorpe, published by Hodder and Stoughton
The popular guide to the law is updated to coincide with the introduction of Citizenship into the National Curriculum.
30 free copies were sent to every secondary school in England and Wales, courtesy of the Home Office and the Duke of Edinburgh's Award Scheme.
Copies also available from bookshops, price £3.99. ISBN 0-340-846-836
Bulk discounts available from the publisher (01235 827720):

Your Rights and Responsibilities
edited by Don Rowe, published by Evans Brothers (in press)
A new two-part text covering most of the elements of the new Citizenship curriculum.
For more information or to order contact sales@evansbrothers.co.uk.

Judges and Schools – A guide to Court Visits
Available from the Citizenship Foundation

Youth Work and the Promotion of Citizenship
by Don Rowe
The report of research into perceptions of citizenship education amongst professional youth workers, and into which activities are seen as promoting positive, participatory citizenship in the informal sector.
Available from the Citizenship Foundation. Price £8 plus p+p. ISBN 0-953-01853-9.

Citizenship Education – some useful contacts

Many of these are linked to the Citizenship Foundation website www.citfou.org.uk

Amnesty International, 99 Rosebery Ave, London EC1R 4RE
Tel. 020 7814 6200 www.amnesty.org.uk

Anne Frank Trust, PO Box 1180, London N6 4LN Tel. 020 8340 9077 www.annefrank.org.uk

Anti-Slavery International, Thomas Clarkson House, The Stableyard, Broomgrove Road, London SW9 9TL Tel. 020 7501 8920 www.antislavery.org

Centre for Citizenship Studies in Education, University of Leicester, 21 Leicester Road, Leicester LE1 7RF Tel. 0116 2523681 www.le.ac.uk/education/centres/citizenship/cs.html

Changemakers, Baybrook Farm, Lower Goodney, Nr Wells, Somerset BA5 1RZ
Tel. 01458 834767 www.changemakers.org.uk

Charter 88 Democracy/rights and responsibilities/voting/constitution/
18a Victoria Park Square, London E2 9PB Tel. 020 8880 6088 www.charter88.org.uk and www.citizen21.org.uk

Community Service Volunteers, 237 Pentonville Road, London N1 9NJ
Tel. 020 7278 6601 www.csv.org.uk

Development Education Association, 29-31 Cowper St, London EC2A 4AP
Tel. 020 7490 8108 www.dea.org.uk

Education in Human Rights Network, Centre for Global Education, College of Ripon and York St. John, Lord Mayor's Walk, York YO3 7EX
Tel. 01904 656771 www.hrea.org

Global Express Rapid response information series for schools on world events in the news. Rm 2 Panos Institute, 9 White Lion St, London N1 9PD
Tel. 020 7278 1111 www.dep.org.uk/globalexpress

The Hansard Society, St Phillips Building North, Sheffield St, London WC2A 2EX
Tel. 020 7955 7478 www.hansard-society.org.uk

Institute for Citizenship, 62 Marylebone High St, London W1M 3AF
Tel. 020 7935 4777 www.citizen.org

Institute for Global Ethics UK Trust, 3-4 Bentinck St, London W1U 2EE
Tel. 020 7486 1954 www.globalethics.org.uk

JMU Foundation for Citizenship, Liverpool John Moores University, Roscoe Court, 4 Rodney St, Liverpool L1 2TZ Tel. 0151 231 3852 www.livjm.ac.uk/citizen/

Kick It Out Campaign to eradicate racism in football. Unit 3, 1-4 Christine St, London EC2A 4PA Tel. 020 7684 4884 www.kickitout.org

National Youth Agency, 17-23 Albion St, Leicester LE1 6GD
Tel. 0116 285 3700 www.nya.org.uk

Operation Black Vote, 18a Victoria Park Square, London E2 9PB
Tel. 020 8880 6061 www.obv.org.uk

Oxfam Education Unit, 4th floor, 4 Bridge Place, London SW1V 1XY
Tel. 020 7931 7660 www.oxfam.org.uk/coolplanet

Parliamentary Education Unit, Rm 604, Norman Shaw Buildings (N), London SW1A 2TT
Tel. 020 7219 2105 www.explore.parliament.uk

Refugee Council, 3 Bondway, London SW8 1SJ
Tel. 020 7820 3000 www.refugeecouncil.org.uk

Save the Children Fund, 17 Grove Lane, London SE5 8RD
Tel. 020 7703 5400 www.savethechildren.org.uk

School Councils UK, Lawford House, 5 Albert Place, London N3 1QB
Tel. 020 8349 2459 www.schoolcouncils.org

Street Law, Inc. An American organisation dedicated to education about the law, human rights
and democracy. Runs projects to support active citizenship. www.streetlaw.org

The 1990 Trust, National Black organisation set up to protect and pioneer the interests of
Britain's Black communities. Winchester House Rm 12, 9 Cranmer Road, Kennington Park,
London SW9 6EJ Tel. 020 7582 1990 www.blink.org.uk

FALKIRK COUNCIL
LIBRARY SUPPORT
FOR SCHOOLS